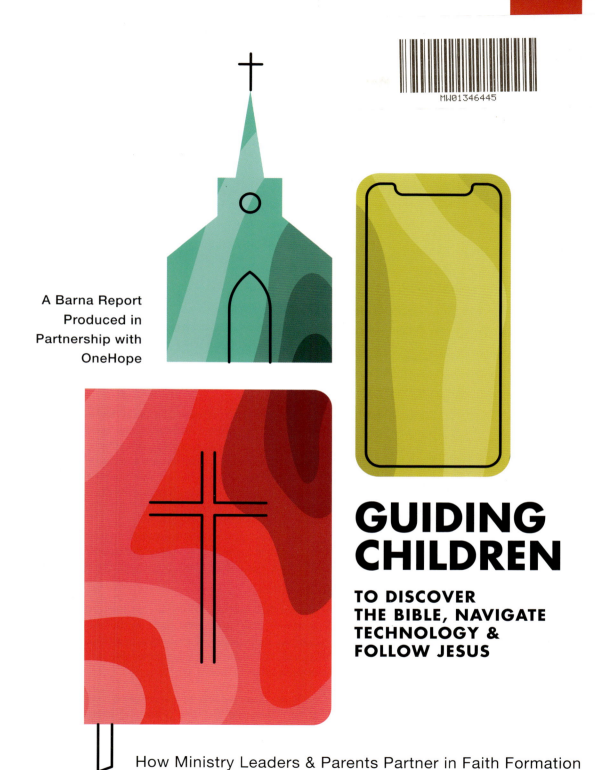

A Barna Report Produced in Partnership with OneHope

GUIDING CHILDREN

TO DISCOVER THE BIBLE, NAVIGATE TECHNOLOGY & FOLLOW JESUS

How Ministry Leaders & Parents Partner in Faith Formation

Copyright © 2020 by Barna Group. All rights reserved.

ISBN: 978-1-945269-46-2

All information contained in this document is copyrighted by Barna Group and shall remain the property of Barna Group. U.S. and international copyright laws protect the contents of this document in their entirety. Any reproduction, modification, distribution, transmission, publication, translation, display, hosting or sale of all or any portion of the contents of this document is strictly prohibited without written permission of an authorized representative of Barna Group.

The information contained in this report is true and accurate to the best knowledge of the copyright holder. It is provided without warranty of any kind: express, implied or otherwise. In no event shall Barna Group or its respective officers or employees be liable for any special, incidental, indirect or consequential damages of any kind, or any damages whatsoever resulting from the use of this information, whether or not users have been advised of the possibility of damage, or on any theory of liability, arising out of or in connection with the use of this information.

Unless otherwise indicated, all Scripture quotations are taken from the Holy Bible, New Living Translation, copyright © 1996, 2004, 2015 by Tyndale House Foundation. Used by permission of Tyndale House Publishers, Inc., Carol Stream, Illinois 60188. All rights reserved.

Scripture quotations marked (NIV) are taken from the Holy Bible, New International Version®, NIV®. Copyright © 1973, 1978, 1984, 2011 by Biblica, Inc.™ Used by permission of Zondervan. All rights reserved worldwide. www.zondervan.com The "NIV" and "New International Version" are trademarks registered in the United States Patent and Trademark Office by Biblica, Inc.™

Funding for this research was made possible by the generous support of OneHope. Barna Group was solely responsible for data collection, analysis and writing of the report.

5	**PREFACE**
	by Rob Hoskins, OneHope
11	**INTRODUCTION**
15	**1. CHANGING LANDSCAPES**
37	**2. DISCOVERING SCRIPTURE**
53	**3. CHURCH FAMILIES**
71	**CONCLUSION**
	APPENDIX
75	A. NOTES
76	B. METHODOLOGY
78	**ACKNOWLEDGEMENTS**
79	**ABOUT THE PROJECT PARTNERS**

By Rob Hoskins, *OneHope President*

I'm excited about this generation. Even more so since becoming a grandpa. When I found out I was becoming a grandparent, everything changed... and yet nothing changed.

Everything changed in that what I've been doing for the entirety of my life and ministry—reaching children and youth with the truth of God's Word—became deeply personal. Now I wake up at night not only thinking about the 113 million children and youth we're reaching this year through OneHope, but also thinking about the world my granddaughter is going to grow up in.

As I step into this new responsibility as a grandparent to help my baby granddaughter become ready to face that world, three things stand out to me from Jesus' baptism in the Jordan river that prepared him to go out and start his ministry.

> At that moment heaven was opened, and he saw the Spirit of God descending like a dove and alighting on him. And a voice from heaven said, "This is my Son, whom I love; with him I am well pleased."
> *(Matt. 3:16–17, NIV)*

Our job as guides to the next generation is to endow our young people with:

1. **IDENTITY** (*"This is my son"*) so they know who they are in Christ.
2. **AFFIRMATION** (*"whom I love, with him I am well pleased"*) of who they are becoming, being in close proximity and relationship so we can be their biggest cheerleaders and know what's important to them, encouraging and affirming decisions in their life.

③ **LOVE FOR GOD'S WORD** (*"It is written"*) so that when they are tempted by the world, like Jesus was tempted by Satan in the desert, they respond grounded in the truth of God's Word.

Pastors, leaders, teachers, parents: We are to help young people establish their divine identity in Christ, surround them with a community that builds authentic relationships and help them hide God's Word in their hearts. Then, no matter what life throws their way, they will be rooted and will know where to turn for truth, answers, support and encouragement.

While becoming a grandpa changed something in me, what didn't change is my calling. We as parents, grandparents, children's pastors, youth leaders and teachers have a tremendous responsibility. It's the same responsibility we've always had in every generation:

> And you must commit yourselves wholeheartedly to these commands that I am giving you today. Repeat them again and again to your children. Talk about them when you are at home and when you are on the road, when you are going to bed and when you are getting up. Tie them to your hands and wear them on your forehead as reminders. Write them on the doorposts of your house and on your gates.
> *(Deut. 6:6–9)*

Yes, we are facing unique challenges. But we also have access to amazing new tools and opportunities. I truly believe that this is a great day for us to engage young people with God's Word in new ways.

Toddlers and teens have ubiquitous access to information, but they still need adults to help them translate knowledge into wisdom. We are to be the guardrails helping the next generation navigate this knowledge-rich world and the struggles that come with growing up.

Scripture engagement, faith community and positive family experiences work together to develop spiritually vibrant children with resilient faith.

The need for Scripture engagement in the upbringing of today's youth hasn't changed; how they can access and experience the story for themselves has. We've seen an overwhelming response to digital Scripture-engagement tools like the *Bible App for Kids* and other programs. It's our job to fully leverage all the great tools we have, once we know where our children and youth are, and meet them there.

To help with that, we believe research is revelatory. It holds up a mirror that allows us to understand our times and either reinforces that we are doing good, effective, fruitful ministry in the reality in which we are living—or lets us know what needs to change.

What you will find in the pages of this report is meant to give a glimpse into the current reality of the new generation, to identify gaps and to celebrate areas of growth. We are excited to share research that will prompt conversations around the most influencing factors in the lives of young people so that pastors, leaders, teachers and parents can unite and work together to nurture a deep, robust and lasting faith in the next generation.

> O my people, listen to my instructions.
> Open your ears to what I am saying . . .
> We will not hide these truths from our children;
> we will tell the next generation
> about the glorious deeds of the Lord . . .
> so the next generation might know them—
> even the children not yet born—
> and they in turn will teach their own children.
> So each generation should set its hope anew on God,
> not forgetting his glorious miracles
> and obeying his commands.
> *(Ps. 78:1, 4, 6–7)*

Parents

Engaged Christian Parents
U.S. adults who are the parent of at least one child ages 6 to 12 and identify as Protestant, Catholic or other Christian, who have attended church within the past month, agree strongly that the Bible is the inspired Word of God and that Jesus was crucified and raised, have made a personal commitment to him that is important, and desire to pass along their faith to their child. All participants in this study qualified under this definition.

Media-Stressed Parents
Engaged Christian parents who rank at least two media-related issues in their top three struggles related to their child's faith formation. (Media-related issues include inappropriate internet searches, digital content such as YouTube and Netflix, video games and social media.)

Self-Guided Parents
Engaged Christian parents who say they rely most on themselves for their child's faith development and do not rank their church's leaders among their top two resources to rely on.

Church-Guided Parents
Engaged Christian parents who say they rely most on their church's leaders for their child's faith development, and do not rank themselves among their top two resources to rely on.

Resource Parents
Engaged Christian parents who report using at least one of the resource types included in the survey *and* say they want training from their church's leaders on how to talk about sensitive topics with their children.

Children

Media-Engaged Children
Engaged Christian parents report their child spends 16 or more hours each week using media (TV, computer, mobile or gaming device) *for entertainment*. (Less media-engaged children consume fewer than 16 hours of entertainment media per week, according to their parents.)

Bible-Engaged Children
Engaged Christian parents report their child engages at least weekly with the Bible in some form. (Less Bible-engaged children do not engage at least weekly with the Bible.)

Church-Engaged Children
Engaged Christian parents report their child attends church weekly or more often. (Less church-engaged children attend less frequently.)

Family-Engaged Children
Engaged Christian parents report their child spends over 13 hours a week with family in conversation or play, including mealtimes, family activities, etc. (Less family-engaged children spend less time with their family.)

KEY FINDINGS

- The vast majority of engaged Christian parents are satisfied with their child's spiritual development thus far (57% very, 40% somewhat).

- Parents who bring their family to church weekly are more likely to be very satisfied with their child's spiritual development (61%).

- More than half chose their current church primarily because of the children's program (58%).

- Nearly 9 out of 10 parents want their church involved in some capacity in sensitive conversations with their child (88%).

- 8 out of 10 parents say their child engages with the Bible on their own at least once a week (81%). This brings a host of benefits, according to the data.

- 3 out of 4 parents are not yet using any digital resources to help their child engage with the Bible.

- Engaged Christian parents report their children consume much less entertainment media each week than the general population: 8 hours on average vs. 42 hours.[1]

- Even so, one-third are "media-stressed" (34%)—they name two or more media issues among their greatest parenting struggles.

In one of the best-known episodes of Jesus' life, children were brought to him to be blessed, only to be stopped short by his disciples. Perhaps they were trying to keep the children out of his way while he was teaching, but Jesus' response is one of the most beautiful statements about kids in all of Scripture: "Let the children come to me. Don't stop them! For the Kingdom of Heaven belongs to those who are like these children" (Matt. 19:14).

In a literal sense, children are the future of our church and our culture, and few more strategic ministry investments can be made than in children. **Christians who shape the spiritual lives of children are shaping the spiritual landscape of the future.**

But there are challenges as we seek to lead children to Jesus. Today we teach, lead and parent children against the backdrop of a complex culture. Rapid social changes mean we must deal with hard questions at younger ages and earlier stages of development. The ubiquity of screens and everywhere-you-go technology has reshaped the experience of childhood, often in disturbing ways. There are high expectations and commitments of the time and energy of families, which impact traditional understandings of faith formation and shared life.

All of these factors combine to form a new reality for children and their caregivers—a reality characterized by rapid, ongoing change and often manifesting as tension. It can be exhausting to consider how to help a young person grow up today. How can we do it well?

Even in the chorus of opinion that surrounds us, we can find reliable guides—authoritative voices with wisdom for this moment. We have a broad community of Christians facing the same challenges and the timeless principles of Scripture—the ultimate guide to becoming the kind of grownups who guide kids to resilient faith.

After all, while many elements of childhood today feel dramatically different from previous decades, childhood itself hasn't changed. Kids are still kids. They pass through the same developmental stages, experience the same joys, frustrations and longings to belong. They still need parents and guardians. They still look up to adults in their faith community. Are we raising them in new realities? Yes. But passing on the faith is an ancient calling—see the passage from Deuteronomy cited above—and it hasn't changed as much as we might think.

With this goal in mind, three key dynamics emerge for Christians to understand and interact with: the changing landscape of tech and media, the vital role Bible engagement plays in spiritual formation, and the ongoing importance of church and communities of faith.

To better understand the dynamics shaping childhood faith formation today, Barna was commissioned by OneHope to study three groups with different viewpoints: engaged Christian parents, children's ministry leaders, and an eclectic mix of experts in the fields of child development, education, toy and game design, and technology. Researchers define "engaged Christian parents" as follows: They have attended a Christian church service within the past month (other than for a holiday or a special event); they strongly agree that the Bible is the inspired Word of God and contains truth about the world; they believe Jesus Christ was crucified and raised from the dead to conquer sin and death; they have made a personal commitment to Jesus Christ that is still important in their life today; and they desire to pass faith on to their child. In addition to qualifying under that definition, study participants are also the parent of at least one child age 6 to 12.

In addition to parent data and analysis, this report features insights from an array of church leaders and other practitioners and thinkers. They don't always agree with each other, but their unique perspectives tease important nuance from the quantitative research among parents.

Some data points in this study will prompt ministry leaders and parents to pause and consider the implications for the kids in our orbit. But many findings also give us reason to hope. **While the culture is changing rapidly, God is not.** And he invites us through the Spirit of Jesus to continue raising up irreplaceable young members of his Kingdom.

The overall image that emerges from the research is that of a *guided journey*. Children need help, as they always have, to navigate the strange and sometimes forbidding landscape of growing up. And cultural changes mean that children must discover who they are in a setting that is often less childhood-friendly than we would wish. But they are not alone. With good caregivers around them—who also have wise guides—there is abundant hope that kids can navigate the journey of early life well, setting them up for long-term faithfulness and a legacy as agents of real renewal and spiritual faith.

Let's explore the findings together.

TOP PARENTING STRUGGLES

Engaged Christian parents rank the following issues among their top three struggles when it comes to guiding their children's spiritual formation.

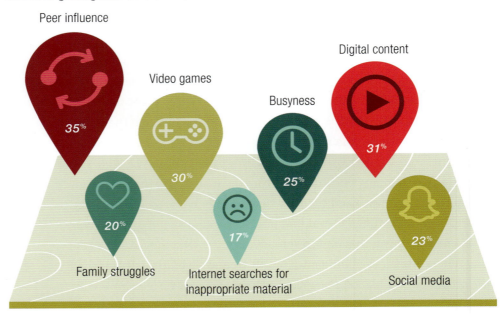

- Peer influence 35%
- Video games 30%
- Busyness 25%
- Digital content 31%
- Family struggles 20%
- Internet searches for inappropriate material 17%
- Social media 23%

Some Struggle More

A few groups of parents express more concern than others when it comes to these issues—including some whose children consume 16 or more hours of entertainment media per week.

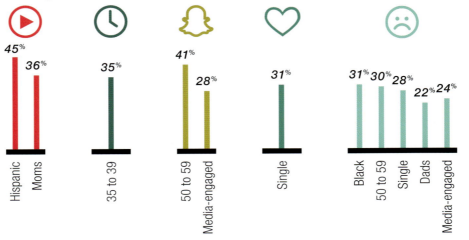

- Hispanic 45%, Moms 36%
- 35 to 39: 35%
- 50 to 59: 41%, Media-engaged 28%
- Single 31%
- Black 31%, 50 to 59 30%, Single 28%, Dads 22%, Media-engaged 24%

1. CHANGING LANDSCAPES

The world has experienced a technological upheaval unlike anything in previous human history. There are people living today who remember the advent of television, who can now tuck a smartphone into their pocket that contains more computing power than all the Allied forces in World War II.

Over the past century, the rate of technological advance has increased exponentially—and with that increase, social opportunities and dilemmas tethered to tech have also multiplied.

Parents and ministry leaders today face many of the same challenges as past generations. How do we help children grow into thriving, productive adults? How do we help them steer away from destructive influences and toward their truest and most rooted selves? How do we encourage them to choose a genuine faith in Jesus for themselves?

Ubiquitous tech and media haven't created many problems; rather, they have amplified—often dramatically—old pressures. Distraction, pornography, bullying and information addiction are all ancient problems. But when the world can fit in your pocket, they become all but inescapable.

Children feel these pressures keenly. Rates of youth anxiety, depression and suicide are climbing sharply[2], just more evidence that the childhood years are no longer a refuge from the pressures of the world as they once were.

What governs the media lives of Christian kids? What dangers and opportunities do parents perceive in the remarkable innovations of the past few decades? What are their pain points as they try to pass on faith to their children? In this chapter, we examine the trends affecting engaged Christian families and their relationship to the changing landscape of technology.

Media in Family Life

Barna asked parents to estimate the number of hours per week their child engages in different activities. There are outliers on both ends of the scale, but here are the median reported number of hours for each activity among engaged Christian families:

- Spend time with family in conversation or play: *10 (hours / week)*
- Use media *for entertainment*: *8*
- Read books: *3*
- Participate in extracurricular activities: *3*
- Attend church activities: *3*
- Search for info online on any device: *2*
- Socialize with other children in person: *1*

Parents in this study are significantly below national averages reported elsewhere when it comes to the number of hours they say their children use media for entertainment. For example, family education nonprofit Common Sense Media pegs average hours among kids ages 8 to 12 at six *per day*.[3] Since children this age tend not to be under constant supervision, some parents may not realize how much media their child is consuming. It's also quite possible that some engaged Christians are more vigilant than the U.S. average when it comes to their child's entertainment consumption.

Regardless of how many hours their children spend on various devices, researchers wanted to understand how engaged Christian parents perceive the impact of media on their child's faith formation. Barna asked parents to rank a variety of issues according to how great a struggle it is for their parenting and discipleship efforts. (The infographic on page 14 examines the areas where parents say they struggle most.) Analysts call those who rank at least two media issues among their top three struggles "media-stressed parents." (Media issues include inappropriate internet searches, digital content such as YouTube and Netflix, video games and social media.)

One-third of engaged Christian parents is media-stressed (34%). As we might expect, given that younger children are less likely to have unmediated access to entertainment media, media-stressed parents are somewhat more apt to have older children (57% ages 10–12 vs. 43% ages 6–9). It follows, then, that older parents—who are more likely than parents in their 20s to have older, plugged-in kids—would likewise be more prone to this kind of anxiety. And in fact parents 50 and older *are* more apt to be media-stressed (43%) than parents 24–34 (29%). Again, this may be due in part to their children's ages, but another factor could be greater discomfort or limited facility with new technologies. Young parents are digital natives themselves and often adopt and adapt to new devices, apps and content without much trouble. But such ease is less likely the case with parents over 50; **older parents may need coaching and guidance to stay informed about their child's media consumption.** There is an opportunity here for churches to partner with faithful-but-uncertain parents.

Media-stressed parents are more likely to say their child uses 16 or more hours of entertainment per week. Barna describes this group of kids as "media-engaged." Thirty-five percent of media-stressed

Changing Childhood
By Beth Cunningham

Imagination allows children to learn creativity. Sadly, we're seeing fewer children who are truly imaginative because all they've ever experienced is being told what to do to be entertained. Children need boredom and nonscheduled time. If their time outside school is packed with activities like music, dance and sports, they won't have the opportunity to learn how to get along with their peers and resolve conflict.

Our culture of always-on, always-connected busyness is shrinking the space we need to cultivate imagination. This is a challenge for today's parents, because other parents are always encouraging them to sign their kids up for something. But our kids *need* downtime—time left to just play. Otherwise, we tell our children to go outside to play, and they return in two minutes, knock on the door and say, "I don't have anything to do. I don't know what to do." And they truly *don't*, because we haven't allowed them the practice a child needs to become imaginative.

Changing Landscapes

parents report their child is media-engaged, compared to one-quarter of parents who are not media stressed (26%).

Further, parents who do not rank *any* media issues among their top struggles (41% of all engaged Christian parents) are more likely than those who are media-stressed to say their child takes in just six or fewer hours of entertainment per week (48% vs. 37%). In sum, there is at least

Children today are being exposed to mature materials and topics at a younger age than they used to be, due to tech use. For example, it's not uncommon for a nine- or ten-year-old in our ministry to be much more aware of pop culture than children her same age 10 years ago.

We also notice elementary school children experiencing more anxiety. Years ago, similar levels of anxiety weren't appearing until kids were in middle or high school. But today, many younger children are expressing worry, from relational stress to bad financial situations at home to their parents' conflicted relationships.

Our church works to create a safe space for children who are carrying burdens they aren't prepared for. They need to share what's going on in their hearts. We create time for them to talk in their small groups at the end of the service and write down on prayer cards how we can be praying for them. Articulation helps—letting them feel heard by caring adults.

Younger parents want community. They long to relate to their tribe. As a ministry, we want to tap into that need for community and provide opportunities for it to grow. One way we've encouraged that is through the formation of supper clubs with groups of 10 parents. That less-formal relational connection meets a deep felt need that parents share. ●

BETH CUNNINGHAM *is children's pastor at Church of the Highlands in Alabama, which ministers to preschool to fifth grade children across 18 campuses. She has served on church staff for more than 20 years. She is married to Shon and they have two children.*

some correlation between a parent's media stress level and their child's volume of entertainment consumption.

However, **it may be valuable to reflect more on *how* kids spend their screen time than on *how much* time they spend—whether active or passive, social or isolated, creating or merely consuming.** Media issues are not only about the scope or scale of screen time; among other things, they also relate to the issue of peer influence—because, thanks to their mobile devices, kids (especially older ones) bring peers with them everywhere. Different parents have different challenges, but an overall plurality ranks peer influences (35%) and digital content (31%) among their top three struggles.

Changing media behavior may offer young people respite from tough peer situations, but it is unlikely to fix them altogether. The greatest felt need of parents comes back to a "people problem," one that is familiar to every generation. In the varied and competing pressures of social life, how can young people be encouraged to make healthy and informed choices and relationships?

Unsurprisingly, media-engaged children are more likely than others to engage the Bible through some kind of digital technology, whether by app (37% weekly

Continued on page 21

Developing for Good
A Q&A with Dan Scott

You believe 11 is a key age in a child's development. Why?

Eleven is a "magic age" because a child's brain is getting ready for adulthood and becomes malleable again. If you were to look at a scan of a two-year-old's or a three-year-old's brain and compare it to a scan of an 11-year-old's, the scans look the same. Very similar monumental developmental shifts are happening.

At ages two and three, a child's brain is getting ready to learn. They're starting to put sentences together and are learning fine motor skills. The 11-year-old is entering puberty. It's the best time to teach a child what they need to know, because a lot of formative memories happen at age 11 and into the preteen years. It's also when our brains get rid of what we don't need or use, a process called "cognitive pruning."

How does this relate to teaching kids about faith?

Church leaders need to understand

that kids are not remembering what they learned in Sunday school from week to week, *because they don't use it*. To help things "stick," we need to partner with parents and encourage them to continue the conversation with their kids.

Eleven is an age when kids can handle more abstract thought, but in spite of this growth in abstract thinking, there still need to be concrete "handles." If there aren't, a small-group discussion time could still result in a roomful of crickets, because 11-year-olds haven't had a concrete experience on which to base an abstract conversation. For example, if we're teaching about the idea of grace, we can talk to kids about presents and how grace is a gift. We can ask them, "How do you feel when you get an unexpected gift from someone?" That provides them with a concrete experience they can attach grace to. Then we can explain, "Salvation is an unexpected gift that God gives us through Jesus." The more concrete experiences teachers can use to relate to kids, the better abstract conversations will go.

How can churches help kids use tech for good?

What if church became the place where kids were taught to use technology to learn about their faith? For example, I love questions and believe the church needs to be the safest place to ask any question possible. So in a small group setting, if someone has a question, the leader can model a positive use of technology by saying, "Let's look it up together!"

Church should meet people where they are. Kids are already on YouTube, so the church should be on YouTube producing videos on relevant topics. Churches can also help parents understand what's happening at church by connecting to them on Facebook and Instagram. We can also use technology to connect kids to Scripture. Leaders can use a Bible app from stage instead of a printed Bible and show kids that in the palm of their hand, they already have the Bible in every possible translation. The more we can point kids to what's *good* about technology, and how they can use technology to grow their faith, the better. ●

DAN SCOTT *is the director for 252 Kids and 252 Preteen curriculum at Orange. He has worked with kids for over 20 years as a teacher, pastor and communicator. He and his wife, Jenna, have four children.*

Child Consumes 16 or More Media Hours Per Week, Media-Stressed vs. Not Media-Stressed Parents

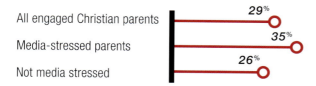

All engaged Christian parents — 29%
Media-stressed parents — 35%
Not media stressed — 26%

n=506 U.S. engaged Christian parents with at least one child age 6 to 12, Sept.–Oct. 2018.

vs. 27% less engaged children), audio (27% weekly vs. 17%) or video (27% weekly vs. 21%). These data point to opportunities for greater biblical engagement among media-engaged kids and media-stressed parents! After all, these are highly engaged Christians; their faith is much more than nominal. **They *long* for their kids to love Jesus passionately and live lives patterned around faithfulness to the Gospel—but they need the right resources in order to be knowledgeable guides.**

Generally speaking, parents of media-engaged children lean more heavily on the church to provide them with stability and resources for their child's spiritual growth. Media-engaged kids are significantly more likely to attend Christian camp (38% vs. 26% less media) and to attend Sunday school or children's church (83% vs. 73%). Part of this correlation is likely due to age: Media-engaged kids are usually older. But it's also possible that some parents whose children are consuming a lot of entertainment media have a sense of urgency to get them into Christian social circles, leaning more heavily on the church to meet faith-formation needs. Parents as well as children need connection and guidance for how to relate to tech and media in a healthy way for their family.

How can the church be a sorely needed guide for parenting children well when it comes to technology? How can parents find the camaraderie and resources they need to make a potent impact on their kids during their formative years?

Play & Generation YouTube

A Q&A with Rod Hudnut

How have you seen the ways kids relate to resources and entertainment shift in recent years?

YouTube is now the number-one brand for kids 2 to 11. As a result, companies are designing entire toy or media brands around what looks good on a short "unboxing" video or something similar. The big experiment we're all in the midst of is what it means for kids to be so screen-addicted from such an early age. You see it all the time in restaurants: Two-year-olds whose parents just hand them a phone to keep them quiet. How will our brains wire differently when they're so digitally connected and influenced?

Is there anything different about how kids play today versus 25 years ago?

Yes and no. In the toy business we see enduring ways that kids play in order to grow. Play is essential to development. So there's hair play and clothes play, transformation play, storytelling play, racing play and a host of other categories we recognize. Those patterns will remain evergreen. What's changing is how many of these play patterns kids now engage with *digitally*. Children 30 years ago would play with He-Man and tell stories, and that's how they got their battle action play out. Now they get it online with Fortnite or some other game.

The outcomes of this will intensify as virtual reality becomes more of a factor in culture. A video game is a more intense emotional experience than playing with action figures—and virtual reality is a more intense experience than playing video games. And of course there are ethical implications.

But change is like a knife. You grab it by the handle or you grab it by the blade. And if we grab it by the handle, we can use it to do something useful. There is opportunity here. To return to YouTube, we have nearly unlimited ability to reach young people in their own "language." What would it mean to effectively engage that space for good and the message of Jesus?

Culture changes. When it does, Christianity needs to both stay the same *and* reach people in ways that speak to them today. ●

Parents' Approaches to Faith Formation

The level of satisfaction that engaged Christian parents feel related to their child's spiritual formation is quite high overall. Fifty-seven percent feel "very" satisfied. Combining them with the 40 percent who feel "somewhat" satisfied, we find that few parents (just 3%) report being dissatisfied with their child's spiritual formation. (Of course, parents' levels of reported satisfaction may or may not be evidence of a child's actual spiritual health or wellbeing.)

Continued on page 27

Satisfaction with Child's Spiritual Formation

- Very satisfied
- Somewhat satisfied
- Somewhat dissatisfied
- Very dissatisfied

57%
40%
2%
1%

n=506 U.S. engaged Christian parents with at least one child age 6 to 12, Sept.–Oct. 2018.

Parental satisfaction is not the same as lasting faith formation, but family faith engagement *can* make a lasting difference, as David Kinnaman explores in *Faith for Exiles*.

ROB HUDNUT *is one of the most innovative and prolific storytellers in children's entertainment. For nearly 20 years he created movies and TV series for Barbie, Hot Wheels, American Girl and many other Mattel characters and brands. Today his company creates original faith-based kids programing. He advises animation studios, toy companies and toy inventors on play-based storytelling.*

TWEENS PULL BACK

In families with *only* tweens (10 to 12) and only younger children (6 to 9),* analysts find evidence that older kids pull back from regular Bible engagement. Yet this tween phase is catalytic for faith that lasts.

6- to 9-year-old   10- to 12-year-old

How often does your child engage with the Bible on their own?

● 4 or more times a week   ● A few times a week   ○ Once a week

Printed book

Storybook Bible

Bible app

Audio version
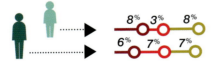

Video version
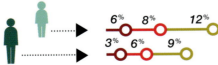

*In order to isolate the effects to these age groups, analysts pulled out parents with kids in both age groups. The above data shows, for example, parents with a 6 to 9-year-old but not a 10 to 12-year-old and vice versa. These families may have other aged children, however - older than 12 or younger than 6. | n = 218 parents of 6- to 9-year-olds and n = 195 parents of 10- to 12-year-olds.

Families spend less time engaging with Scripture together as their children reach the tween stage. In particular, discussions about the Bible decline significantly among households with 10- to 12-year-olds, as shown below. However, when multiple children are present in a household, families more commonly engage with the Bible altogether.

Parents also less commonly use resources—except classes or activities—as kids move into the tween stage.

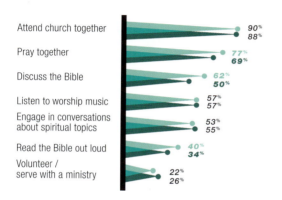

Do together as a family, at least once a week:

Attend church together	90%	88%
Pray together	77%	69%
Discuss the Bible	62%	50%
Listen to worship music	57%	57%
Engage in conversations about spiritual topics	53%	55%
Read the Bible out loud	40%	34%
Volunteer / serve with a ministry	22%	26%

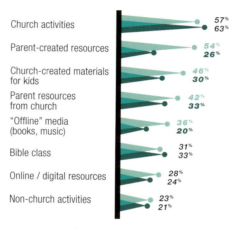

Resources parents use to help their child(ren) engage with the Bible:

Church activities	57%	63%
Parent-created resources	54%	26%
Church-created materials for kids	46%	30%
Parent resources from church	42%	33%
"Offline" media (books, music)	36%	20%
Bible class	31%	33%
Online / digital resources	28%	24%
Non-church activities	23%	21%

Colored numbers are significantly different.

Kids' interest in attending church starts to change. In the early years, children's interest in attending church grows, but when they hit their tweens, kids shift. As they emerge into their teens, kids seem to split into those who engage more in church and those who lose interest.

Child's interest in attending church, past few years

○ Less interested ○ No change in interest ○ More interested

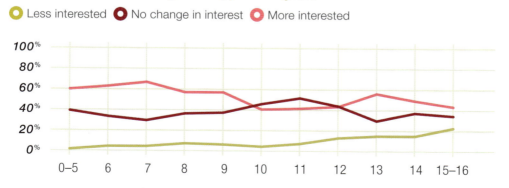

25

Available for Connection

By Hettie Brittz

The way our children's brains are primed for outright enslavement to the online world is hair-raising. In a real sense, we now have to compete spiritually with the input from online sources. We have to figure out how to cut through the noise.

Children now have access to more belief systems, more opinions and more voices than ever before. In the past, though there may have been a few lone voices sending different messages, for the most part parents' voices could be strengthened by what a pastor and a few teachers were saying. Now that has flipped. Most of the voices coming to children are through social media and online activity, and often they don't agree with what parents and churches are communicating. At ages six, seven and eight, kids simply cannot distinguish between these different voices. They don't have the objectivity to judge which voices are worth listening to and which are not.

I absolutely believe the medium influences the message. But I also see that the biggest difference is the *person* facilitating the learning experience. To a child, if Miss Sandy at my church loves me and is happy to see me when I arrive in class, then she can put a black-and-white sheet of paper in front of me any day of the week and I will engage with it. I experience something with my teacher that is very real—more real than the stranger on my iPad.

Yes, our material is important. We need it to be engaging and to communicate all the right foundational truths to guide children in forming their concept of God. But it's the *people*, the facilitators in children's learning, that are key. Often, kids are on their devices because of a lack of emotional connectedness with their parents. It's our unavailability and busyness as parents and educators that make them default to the easy stimulation of a screen. There are very few kids who will remain engaged to a screen if an adult is ready to connect, play, listen or do a fun activity with them. Sadly, all too often we grown-ups are simply not available. ●

HETTIE BRITTZ *is developer of the Evergreen Parenting Course and heads a group of more than 200 facilitators in eight countries who use the course to help families. She is married to the Gospel singer and music producer Louis Brittz, and they have three children.*

What role does a church play in guiding parents in their spiritual formation activities with kids? An important one. When asked where they turn for advice or guidance related to their child's faith development, "my own upbringing" (66%) ranks about equally with "church leadership" (63%) as a top-two choice.

younger parents are likely to have less life experience that is relevant to parenting well. They may also feel more pressure than older adults to "do it right," which

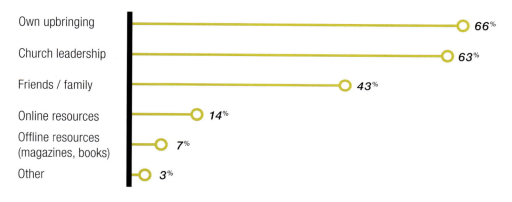

Top Two Guidance Givers

- Own upbringing — 66%
- Church leadership — 63%
- Friends / family — 43%
- Online resources — 14%
- Offline resources (magazines, books) — 7%
- Other — 3%

n=506 U.S. engaged Christian parents with at least one child age 6 to 12, Sept.–Oct. 2018.

A parent's age appears to play a factor in their relationship to church leaders. Looking to ministry leaders for advice is more common among younger parents (69% ages 24–34 and 68% ages 35–39 vs. 60% ages 40–49 and 56% ages 50+). They express a greater need for guidance and mentorship to support their family's spiritual life—which is unsurprising, as

may result in anxiety. Between social media "influencers" who make parenting look easy and glamorous and the ever-expanding plethora of parenting resources and styles competing in the marketplace, some young parents need reassurance and coaching to feel they are enough.

Ministry staff, friends and extended family members are just some of the people, in addition to parents, who influence the minds and hearts of kids. So who or what do engaged Christian parents see as key influences guiding their child's

Continued on page 29

Childhood Wonder

By Trish McClung

Psychologist Lev Vygotsky believed children learn better in a social context with the guidance of a more knowledgeable person who can point things out to them. For example, when you're watching a TV program with a child and say, "Did you see that?" or "Hey, look at that!", learning is happening in a social setting.

This has profound implications in today's world of technology, where kids are able to easily look up and acquire vast amounts of information. Just having access to the facts isn't enough. Kids still need guidance—though it shouldn't necessarily be heavy handed. But they benefit from our pointing things out and asking, "What do you think about that? What do you understand about that? What does that mean to you? How would you interpret that? Is that something you should avoid?" These kinds of questions can help children not only acquire knowledge, but also refine it.

The awe and wonder of kids is still there and always has been. I saw this when we took our eight-year-old grandson to Egypt. When we flew in and he saw the landscape, he exclaimed, "There it is . . . ancient Cairo!" It was incredible to see the sense of awe on his face.

No matter how tech-savvy children are, that natural sense of wonder is present, and we would be wise to tap into it when we're teaching them. Kids love to see things they haven't seen and experienced before. They can still be impressed.

DR. PATRICIA McCLUNG *is Professor in Special Education and Chair of Early Childhood, Elementary and Special Education at Lee University in Cleveland, Tennessee. Her interests and research include the attrition of teachers in the field of special education, the use of narrative inquiry in data collection and analysis, and integrative learning. Trish is married to Alan McClung. They have a married adult daughter and two grandchildren.*

spiritual development? The vast majority of parents fall into one of two categories. Slightly more than half (55%) analysts call "self-guided parents," who rank their own conversations with their children as most important (87%) or as No. 2 (13%). The remaining 44 percent are "church-guided parents," ranking their church as No. 1 (84%) or as No. 2 (16%) without putting *themselves* at the top. Moms and dads of middle-schoolers are significantly more likely than parents with children of other ages to rely on the church (43% vs. 31% who are self-guided).

Leading Sensitive Conversations

Every parent and ministry leader knows the pressure related to broaching a tough but necessary topic with a child or teen. Besides subjects that are often surrounded by shame in our culture, such as sex, addiction, pornography and other "unmentionables," a vast array of topics is presented to young people at increasingly tender ages *because* of tech access: racism, gender identity, public violence, sexual assault and terrorism, among others.

Do engaged Christian parents want their church's help addressing these issues with their children? Sometimes.

Listening Into Community

By Bryan Cheney

Kids 6 to 12 experience a deep need for community but wonder how to connect with other kids. Our culture doesn't emphasize community much any more. Kids used to go play outside in their neighborhoods with other children, but are no longer doing that as much. This matters. Kids come to our services and say they don't have friends at church, because they don't know how to make friends. (Of course, technology plays into this, too.)

This lack of community extends to the family, which just makes the ache worse. When many families go out to dinner with their kids, everyone is on their phone. Relational connections that used to exist within families are eroding.

Churches can begin to respond by *listening*. Our church has a member who designs focus groups for a notable company, and he told us, "Almost any company in the world would pay lots to have access to their end users the way the church does." We have a great

Overall, nearly nine out of 10 parents (88%) say they want their church involved *in some capacity* in sensitive conversations with their child. According to children's and youth ministry leaders Barna interviewed, about one in six parents (17%) expresses reluctance or discomfort when church leaders want to address sensitive topics with young people.

Perhaps counterintuitively, college graduates are *more* likely than less-educated parents to say they want church guidance (94% vs. 84%). This is important for ministry leaders to notice, since it might be tempting to assume that well-educated parents are more equipped opportunity to hear from families—why not take advantage of that?

We've put together focus groups to connect parents who have kids the same ages and make space for them to ask questions. In those groups our church can get a sense for what the real needs are, but can also ask questions in return, like, "What can we do to serve your family? What resources do you need?" Through conversations, we're building trust. We've found that the more we do this, the more engaged parents are and the more credibility we have to speak into their lives. It's reciprocal.

We use this focus group model with kids, too. Twice a month we provide food and have kids come talk to us for a couple of hours about a given topic, such as friendship. We'll say, "We want to talk about friendship. What does it mean to you? What works for you?" In response to the first question we ask, kids will usually give us the answer they think we want. But by the third or fourth question, they'll start providing unbelievably rich answers. Later, kids come up to us and say, "I just thought of something this last week related to friendship" (or whatever topic we've been talking about). Not only are we satisfying their need for community, but we're also keeping them engaged with the topics we're addressing. ●

BRYAN CHENEY *is a Christ-follower, husband, dad and Promiseland Director at Willow Creek Community Church—in that order!*

to broach these topics. At work here could be what one analyst calls "nuance paralysis": reluctance to offer simple answers to complex questions. Well-informed parents may need guidance for what kinds of answers are age-appropriate in their complexity and nuance.

Another factor may be a child's entertainment consumption. Parents of media-engaged children are less likely to say they want to handle sensitive topics by themselves, without any kind of assistance from their church. They are more likely to want training and resources, and to seek multiple trustworthy voices to contribute to the conversation. But they may also need help to recognize that *they* are a vital part of guiding their child through hard topics. They can't simply outsource responsibility to "experts." Rather, they can grow in their own engagement as part of a team of guides that includes church leaders and mentors.

As we might expect, self-guided parents (who primarily rely on themselves for their child's spiritual formation) tend to be more confident in their ability to handle tricky conversations on their own. However, they are no more or less likely than church-guided parents to want church-based training for how to have conversations about these topics.

Intergenerational Community

By Beth Green

Today we sort kids into strict age groups in the classroom and on sports teams. But what seems to be forgotten is the importance of mixed-age groups, including multiple generations. Outside of religious communities, I don't think there's much opportunity for children to interact with older people in shared activities. But I see this as a critical element in children's spiritual formation.

At church, people still interact across generations. I think that's what Paul is encouraging in Titus 2 when he encourages older women to spend time with those who are younger. We all grow when these relationships do! ●

BETH GREEN *is a senior fellow in education for Cardus, and formerly program director of Cardus Education. She is also Visiting Professor of Research, Integration and Educational Formation at Tyndale University College in Toronto.*

Two-thirds of the church-guided group say they want ministry leaders to address sensitive topics with their children (68% vs. 55% self-guided). On the other hand, three in 10 self-guided parents say they don't want sensitive issues addressed at church at all and want to handle them entirely on their own (31% vs. 19% church-guided). These findings may indicate potential disagreements about topic choices in children's or youth programming at church. This is an area where leaders will need to do some digging to find out the dynamics of their specific ministry's families.

At what age do engaged Christian parents and ministry leaders believe kids are exposed to conversations or material related to sensitive social topics? Here's a look at what each group says about four fraught and hard-to-talk-about issues that inevitably arise at some point.

Continued on page 34

When Ministry Leaders & Parents Believe Kids Are Exposed to Pornography

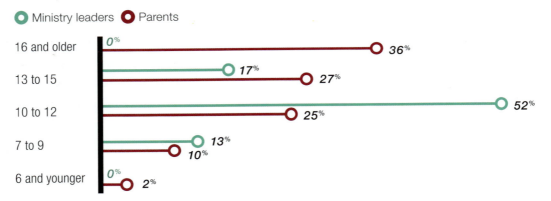

When Ministry Leaders & Parents Believe Kids Are Exposed to Gender Identity

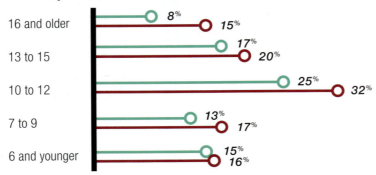

Partnering With Parents
By Brian Dollar

Once kids hit fourth and fifth grades, we're seeing them grapple with what used to be difficult subjects for seventh and eighth graders. They're asking tough questions, especially about who they are. This is why I encourage parents to have age-appropriate discussions about sexuality and gender with their children *before* they reach middle school. Parents can't assume their kids will simply figure things out. If parents wait until later, their kids will have heard about these issues long before.

The church can help by teaching kids that God purposefully and individually designed them, and that they are his masterpiece. If they're able to look at their bodies and personalities from that perspective, and understand the value he says they have, they will be able to avoid a lot of the confusion about identity that's in our society.

Parents want a solid and biblical spiritual experience for their children. Although they may not be able to articulate it, they are also looking for a partner to help train their child in becoming a lifelong follower of Jesus. Certainly some parents understand this better than others, and there are parents who want the church to do it all related to their children's spiritual development. They seem unwilling to do their part to raise their child to follow Jesus. Those parents need help understanding that, for better or worse, spiritual formation happens first and foremost in the home. They are their children's primary spiritual leaders, and the church needs to equip them.

BRIAN DOLLAR *began in kids' ministry in 1992. He loves kids, ministry leaders and everything that involves leading children in their spiritual journey. In 1998 he founded High Voltage Kids Ministry Resources, which creates and provides curriculum, music, games, videos and more to churches around the world. Brian and his wife, Cherith, have two children.*

When Ministry Leaders & Parents Believe Kids Are Exposed to Anxiety, Depression, Suicide

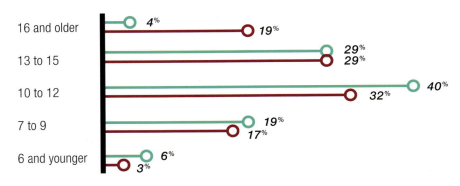

When Ministry Leaders & Parents Believe Kids Are Exposed to Sexual Identity

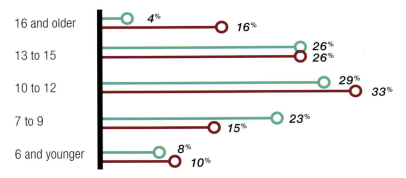

n=506 U.S. engaged Christian parents with at least one child age 6 to 12, Sept.–Oct. 2018;
n=128 U.S. children's ministry leaders; Sep.–Nov. 2018.

The takeaway? **When it comes to social issues, parents and ministry leaders are broadly in agreement about the ages young people encounter sensitive content or topics—except when it comes to pornography.** Ministry leaders are seeing younger kids exposed to porn, while many parents appear to think such exposure comes much later. (Most studies suggest ministry leaders' estimates are closer to the mark.[4])

What is needed is increased communication between parents and children's ministry leaders about what topics are pressing and developmentally appropriate for kids today, and who is best poised to lead those conversations. Children are likely to need more than one guide in these areas, and solidarity between multiple adult figures is likely to be an effective solution to ensure that no child misses vital guidance on an important topic of life.

Media and personal devices come with a host of benefits—connection with others, access to knowledge, opportunities for play and learning—but parents and children need wise guides to navigate tech so that benefits outweigh potential dangers. Faith leaders can start by initiating honest conversations about the impact of new media on young people. **Rather than making mere screen-time reduction the primary goal, intentionality in digital spaces and habits can help Christian families put tech in its proper place.**

Moving toward more intentional media engagement is a countercultural action. This challenge can be an opportunity to meet our neighbors around a shared felt need to discuss and consider these issues together—not just in our churches, but in our living rooms, schools, community centers, and maybe even in our social media feeds.

Thinking Tech Through

By Yu-Kai Chou

Kids today have never experienced a world without a smartphone. But the key question in my mind is whether kids have guides to help them interpret everything. Games, for example: Some are purely violent, or nothing more than "button mashers." They don't spark creativity at all. But other games actually allow for patience, for long-term strategy, for collaboration and many other beneficial things.

But many parents will just take one strategy or another, either saying, "Oh, it's all good so just do whatever you want" or "Hey, it's all evil so stay away from all games." Instead, we should invest time into *thinking through* the pros and cons of the games they are playing, maybe even play with them to provide that guidance. There will be technology no matter what, so the question is if parents are there to guide the context of how children interpret what they are experiencing.

In the end, I feel optimistic about the future, but I feel for the future generation. For kids who don't have good support, teachers, parents and churches giving them the right context, there is a lot to be concerned about. There are so many things distracting them. Their mobile devices are talking, the TV is talking to them, the computer is talking to them. It's so much easier for something negative to reach into their lives, into their hands, into their brains—and so we need to help them lay a solid foundation as *who* they are and not *what* they're holding or seeing. ●

YU-KAI CHOU *is a pioneer in gamification and behavioral design, and author of* Actionable Gamification: Beyond Points, Badges, and Leaderboards. *He has taught at Google, Stanford, LEGO, Tesla, TEDx, and Huawei, among others, and for various governments. He is a Christ-follower and the proud father of twin daughters.*

2 . DISCOVERING SCRIPTURE

"The B-I-B-L-E," goes the old Sunday school hit, "yes, that's the book for me!" Generations of young Christians have proclaimed their readiness to "stand alone on the Word of God"—beginning their discovery of the Scriptures, which St. Augustine called "our letters from home."

The place of the Bible remains central for engaged Christian families today and, as we'll see, regular Bible engagement carries a host of benefits for the spiritual lives of growing kids. But not all parents are sure how to bring the Bible into their family's daily life. They're looking for help and reliable resources from their church community.

Benefits of Bible Engagement

Engaged Christian parents actively involve their children in faith-developing activities, and most are doing a thorough job of it. In fact, eight in 10 report their child engages with the Bible at least weekly (81%). These are "Bible-engaged" families and children. And this single discipline is connected to a host of spiritual benefits. Bible-engaged kids are more likely to engage in a wide spectrum of other spiritual-formation activities. Overall, the data paints a picture of growth guided by God's Word. (See the infographic on the next page.)

Of course, any spiritual picture is bigger than Bible engagement alone. Even children who *don't* engage with the Bible on at least a weekly basis interact with other spiritual formation resources, including

Continued on page 40

ENCOUNTERING THE BIBLE MAKES A BIG DIFFERENCE
to the lives of kids and their families

The data reveals a strong correlation between a child's regular engagement with the Bible and other spiritually formative family activities such as church involvement and prayer. Regular church engagement, while likewise seeming to go hand in hand with spiritual development, does not appear to have as significant an effect as regularly interacting with Scripture.

Child's Bible Engagement
- Bible-engaged (weekly or more often)
- Less Bible-engaged

81%
19%

Child's Church Engagement
- Church-engaged (every week)
- Less church-engaged

61%
39%

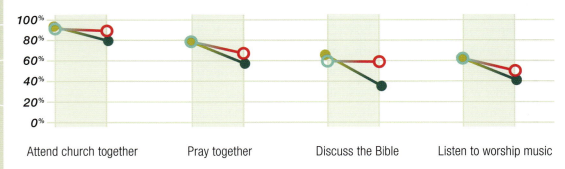

Family activities done together at least once a week

Attend church together | Pray together | Discuss the Bible | Listen to worship music

38

Family activities done together at least once a week

Satisfaction with child's spiritual formation thus far

At least one child older than 12 has made a profession of faith (including baptism, confirmation, first communion, etc.)

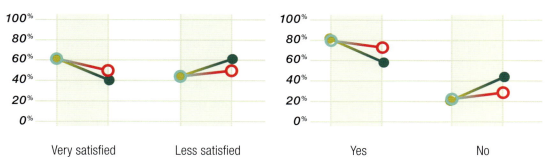

Child's interest in church has *increased* over the past few years

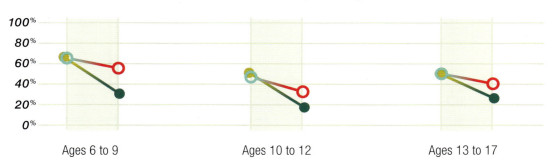

church and extracurricular experiences. However, only two in five parents say they are very satisfied thus far with the spiritual development of their less Bible-engaged child (40% vs. 60% parents of Bible-engaged children). In other words, most parents whose children are *not* regularly engaging with the Bible are aware something is missing from their child's spiritual formation.

Two-thirds of Bible-engaged children attend church every week (66%)—significantly more than less Bible-engaged kids (41% weekly). Add to that two-thirds the 27 percent of Bible-engaged children who have missed only one Sunday in the past month, and a strong link emerges between habits of Bible engagement and of church involvement.

Younger parents are significantly more likely than older parents to report weekly engagement; the consistency across children's ages is notably absent when Bible-engaged kids are sorted by their *parents'* age. Parents over 50 are least likely to report their child is engaging the Bible weekly (67%), and each younger age bracket increases until we see nine out of 10 parents ages 24 to 34 with Bible-engaged kids. Again, younger parents are likelier to have younger children—so they are more apt to engage the Bible alongside their young ones. **Older parents may need a combination of resources and encouragement from church leaders to ensure their life stage (or their older child's) isn't leading to passivity when it comes to leading their family to interact with the Bible.**

Continued on page 42

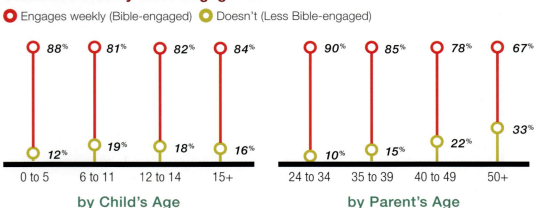

Children's Weekly Bible Engagement

○ Engages weekly (Bible-engaged)   ○ Doesn't (Less Bible-engaged)

by Child's Age

0 to 5	6 to 11	12 to 14	15+
88%	81%	82%	84%
12%	19%	18%	16%

by Parent's Age

24 to 34	35 to 39	40 to 49	50+
90%	85%	78%	67%
10%	15%	22%	33%

n=506 U.S. engaged Christian parents with at least one child age 6 to 12, Sep.–Oct. 2018.

A Worshiping Home

By Davis Carman

Deuteronomy 6 impresses on parents the necessity of diligently teaching our kids how to love God with all of their person. This lesson is to be reinforced constantly: We're told to talk about these things with them when we're at home and when we're walking, when we lie down and when we get up.

In today's world, that might be at the dinner table, in the car or when we're getting up or going to bed. When we intentionally do life together, and read and learn together, we're developing our kids' thinking and putting key topics into their minds. Our kids will start asking us questions we've already prompted through our example.

One of the practical tips I give parents is to have "family worship." Our family called it that (rather than a family devotional time) because we found it changed our whole approach. A devotional time can make parents think, *I've got to find a book to study with the kids, and then I've got to get this time in the schedule and check it off when we're done.* It can quickly become daunting, and some parents are tempted to think, *We missed a couple of nights or a couple of weeks, so we might as well drop it. It's too hard.*

But family worship? That's something much simpler, something you can incorporate into the routine of your day. It might be before breakfast in some seasons of life, or during dinner or before bedtime in others. All it means is that we are choosing to have a short time together to sit down, read the Bible, pray and maybe sing a song or two. It's nothing fancy. But it is important, because it creates a love for God's Word and a love for God himself.

Our children will become aware that this is part of the family routine, just like getting up and making beds and brushing their teeth. This can become a vital part of teaching them to love God and desire to know him more, with all their heart, soul and strength. ●

DAVIS CARMAN *is president of Apologia Educational Ministries. His mission is to help homeschooling families learn, live and defend the Christian faith. He is husband to Rachael and father to seven children.*

Bible-engaged children are deeply involved in their local church. Nearly six in 10 engage in activities other than weekly worship (58% vs. 27%). They are also more likely to participate in Bible studies (37% vs. 9%) and youth group programs (52% vs. 31%).

Overall, children who engage with the Bible at least weekly are more likely to engage with spiritual activities as a family in *every* way. Parents who care about getting their kids into God's Word seem to foster a variety of ways for their family to take the faith journey together.

Hiding the Word in Children's Hearts

By John Murray

It may be "old school," but encouraging kids to memorize Scripture at a young age is a biblical idea. We're to hide the Word in our hearts (Ps. 119:11) and to meditate on it day and night (Josh. 1:8). Parents are told to train up a child (Prov. 22:6), and we're promised that God's Word does not return void (Is. 55:11). Scripture can shape the hearts and minds of kids, and that's why cultivating their hearts for God's Word and training them to love it is so important.

I've seen this in my own life, too. Growing up, I went to public school for first through twelfth grade, but I attended Sunday school and was exposed to Scripture—and it made a profound difference. Yes, I may have memorized Scripture for the wrong reasons sometimes, like to win a prize. But it worked!

I tell teachers not just to have their students memorize Scripture, but to also make sure they understand what that Scripture is saying and how it applies to their lives. This isn't just rote memorization for the sake of memorization. It's about more than the words. ●

JOHN MURRAY *is Founder and President of Imago Dei Leadership Forum (idleadershipforum.org) and a recognized leader in academia who writes and speaks on equipping children and parents to biblically engage modern culture. He and his wife, Barbara, are parents of four Gen Z children.*

Weekly Family Spiritual Activities, by Bible Engagement

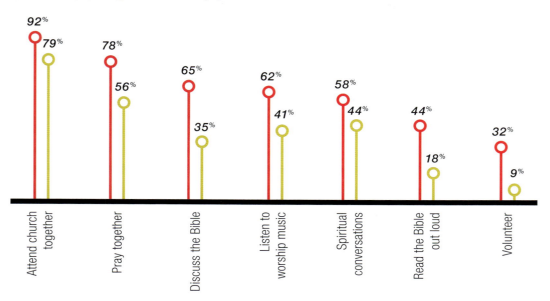

n=506 U.S. engaged Christian parents with at least one child age 6 to 12, Sept.–Oct. 2018.

Volunteerism, spiritual conversations, Bible discussion, church attendance, prayer and more are experienced at higher levels in families where the Bible is read regularly.

Eight out of 10 parents of Bible-engaged kids have at least one child in the household who has made a profession of faith in Jesus, compared to 57 percent whose children interact less with the Scriptures.

Children who engage the Bible weekly are less likely to also be media-engaged kids. (This doesn't necessarily mean that opening the Scriptures reduces screen time—only that there is some correlation between these two factors.) Just 43 percent of Bible-engaged children are also media-engaged, compared to nearly six in 10 less Bible-engaged kids (57%).

In what ways are Bible-engaged families interacting with the Scriptures? In a variety of ways, but most often with a book—right along with families who engage the Bible less often. Fewer than half use other media—so far. (See the following page.)

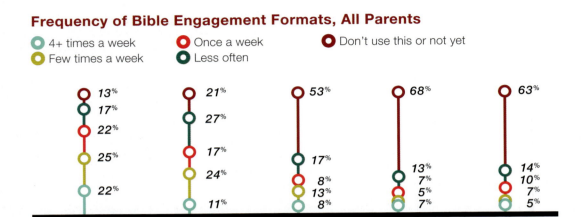

n=506 U.S. engaged Christian parents with at least one child age 6 to 12, Sept.–Oct. 2018.

Reliable Resources

A clear sense of the benefits of Bible engagement, plus high-quality resources that prompt deeper study, can help families continue to grow—and hopefully will help kids stay the course of their Bible habit into adulthood. **The data show a real hunger among engaged Christian parents to get their hands on anything that will help them form faith in their child.**

The parents of Bible-engaged children are more likely than others to look for guidance related to their children's faith development and are less reliant on their own upbringing. (In other words, they are less likely than others to be "self-guided," under Barna's definition.)

They are also open to using faith-formation resources from a variety of sources. If it is high quality, they *will* use it to disciple their kids!

There is significant overlap between the families of Bible-engaged children and a group analysts call "resource parents": those who use at least one of the resources included in the survey *and* who say they want training from church leaders on how to discuss sensitive topics with their child. Eighty-five percent of children with resource parents engage at least weekly with the Bible.

Who & What Parents Rely On for Their Child's Spiritual Formation

○ Bible-engaged ○ Less Bible-engaged

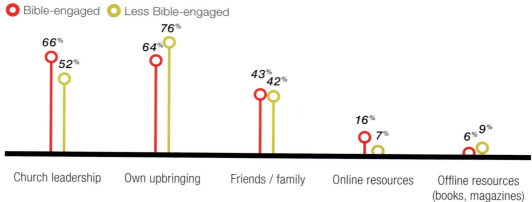

Church leadership	Own upbringing	Friends / family	Online resources	Offline resources (books, magazines)
66% / 52%	64% / 76%	43% / 42%	16% / 7%	6% / 9%

n=506 U.S. engaged Christian parents with at least one child age 6 to 12, Sept.–Oct. 2018.

What Resources Do You Use?

○ Bible-engaged ○ Less Bible-engaged

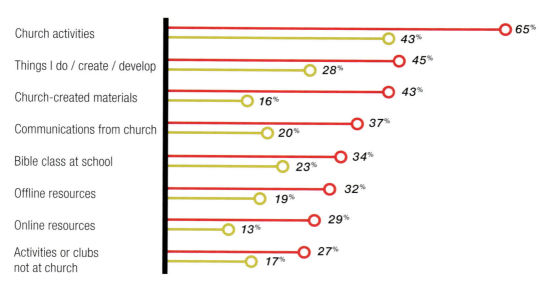

	Bible-engaged	Less Bible-engaged
Church activities	65%	43%
Things I do / create / develop	45%	28%
Church-created materials	43%	16%
Communications from church	37%	20%
Bible class at school	34%	23%
Offline resources	32%	19%
Online resources	29%	13%
Activities or clubs not at church	27%	17%

n=506 U.S. engaged Christian parents with at least one child age 6 to 12, Sept.–Oct. 2018.

Resources Used: All Engaged Christian Parents

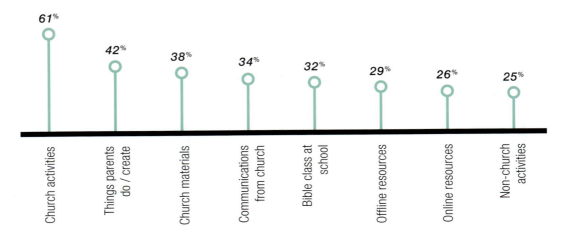

n=506 U.S. engaged Christian parents with at least one child age 6 to 12, Sep.–Oct. 2018.

Resources Used by Resource Parents

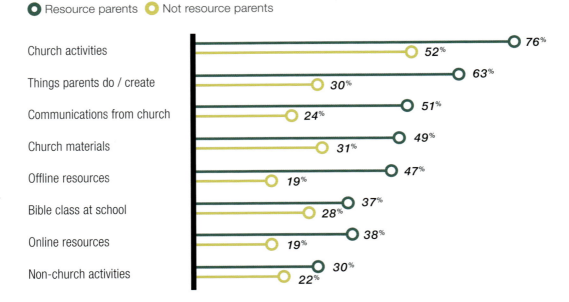

n=506 U.S. engaged Christian parents with at least one child age 6 to 12, Sept.–Oct. 2018.

Children of resource parents are significantly more likely to spend a lot of time with family (47% are family-engaged vs. 30% of non-resource parents), to be avid readers (46% "high books" vs. 34%) and to be very involved with extracurricular activities in their congregation (66% "high church activities" vs. 44%). Resource parents also do more spiritual-formation activities together as a family.

This demonstrates a recursive role for families that interact frequently with church resources. Resource parents want reliable activities and programs from their church's ministries, a desire that drives them to engage in more church activities—and their engagement in church activities increases their trust in their church's resources. (If a church staff is looking for a reason to hire a family curriculum designer, it's right here!) **Both resources and activities play an important role in the faith development of children and youth.**

Resource parents are more likely to agree that the children's programming at their church is the primary reason they attend (64% vs. 54% of non-resource parents). This is not surprising, as it shows receptivity to input and an expectation that there will be value added by the church to their family's faith life.

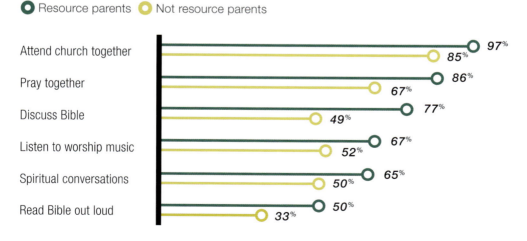

Weekly Family Spiritual Activities, by Resource / Not Resource

● Resource parents ○ Not resource parents

Activity	Resource	Not Resource
Attend church together	97%	85%
Pray together	86%	67%
Discuss Bible	77%	49%
Listen to worship music	67%	52%
Spiritual conversations	65%	50%
Read Bible out loud	50%	33%

n=506 U.S. engaged Christian parents with at least one child age 6 to 12, Sept.–Oct. 2018.

Passing On a Love of Scripture

By Brian Cheney

When adults say something like, "Here's what I'm learning about God, and why I continue to read Scripture," it makes a big impression. They're modeling life-long, humble learning. These kinds of conversations help kids grasp why they need to read the Bible regularly.

If we start the conversation with, "How often do you read your Bible?" kids slip into assignment mode. Instead, we must whet their appetite for Scripture and cultivate their love for it. Then they'll say, "There's a God who loves me. I want to understand that more."

(See bio on page 30.)

In keeping with this theme, three out of four resource parents (74%) look to church leadership as one of the top two influencers of their children's faith development (vs. 56%). Three out of five resource parents want the church to address sensitive topics (61%; 65% want to know *before* such topics are addressed), while only one in five would rather handle tough conversations themselves (20%).

In general, resource parents think their children need exposure to conversations about sensitive topics at younger ages than parents who are more self-guided. For this group of parents—and their kids—guidance and resources from trusted church leaders exert enormous leverage.

Interestingly, though, there is little difference in the level of satisfaction that resource parents and non-resource parents feel about the spiritual development of their children thus far. **There is no one "right" way to encourage a child's faith formation—each spiritual journey looks a little different, and that's okay.** For most kids, parents are the irreplaceable guides for their Christian walk. For some, it will be a teacher, a pastor or a church volunteer. What matters is that there is an emotionally and spiritually available adult with wisdom and resources to support their growing faith in Jesus.

A key part of guiding a child to well-formed faith in Jesus is consistently high Bible engagement. There are a host of benefits enjoyed by Bible-engaged kids, including tighter bonds to their church community, high engagement with

Christian extracurricular activities, a high degree of faith profession and less media consumption.

While delivery methods for Bible engagement can vary, what's clear is that Christian leaders and parents should continue to see the Bible as central to a well-formed childhood faith, encouraging deep connection, at least on a weekly basis, among the young people in their family, church or community.

Additionally, there are significant benefits when parents partner with their church by adopting resources for their home faith life. Along with the Bible, one of the most significant ways parents can help guide their children to a robust faith is using quality resources from *outside* the home to prompt and encourage Christian engagement *inside* the home.

Wiring the House

By Connie Musselman

I like to think of our role as parents and teachers with an electrical metaphor: We wire the house, but it's the Holy Spirit who flips the switch on. We can set up systems and structures for God to use—but it's his truth and power that will make them "come to life."

We never know when God will use something these children have memorized from his Word, so it's exciting to know that thirty years from now, what we're teaching them could have a huge impact in their lives. I believe there are future leaders in our class of three-year-olds, people who will lead their generation. What an honor to serve them as they grow.

As we do this wiring, reaching parents is vital—and in particular mothers, who often have a special role with their kids. I'll often say to gathered groups of moms, "Add up the number of children represented by the mothers sitting at your table." It never fails to amaze me. Connecting with parents is an incredibly strategic way to impact kids—strong wiring that God will use. ●

CONNIE MUSSELMAN *is director of children's ministry at Church of the Apostles in Atlanta and mother to four children.*

TOUGH TALKS

A plurality of engaged Christian parents feel equipped and capable to talk to their children about spiritual topics, but some groups feel varying levels of insecurity or confidence when it comes to talking faith with their children.

All   Moms   Dads
24 to 34   35 to 39   40 to 49   50+

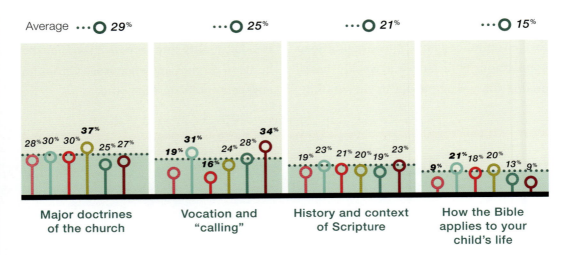

Average ⋯ 29%   ⋯ 25%   ⋯ 21%   ⋯ 15%

Major doctrines of the church: 28% 30% 30% 37% 25% 27%
Vocation and "calling": 19% 31% 16% 24% 28% 34%
History and context of Scripture: 19% 23% 21% 20% 19% 23%
How the Bible applies to your child's life: 9% 21% 18% 20% 13% 9%

Take It to Church?

When it comes to discussing sensitive topics at church, parents are generally open to leaders bringing them up with their kids—at an age appropriate level. Interestingly, parents who say their kids use a high level of entertainment media are more likely to want help from church leaders.

"I want our children's leader to approach these issues at an age-appropriate level."

 62% / 66% / 60%

"I would like to know before our children's leader discusses any of these topics."

 47% / 57% / 43%

Spiritual topics parents find hard to explain / feel uncomfortable talking about

Having a relationship with Jesus	Sin and forgiveness	The authority of the Bible	None of these
Average 13%	12%	11%	42%
9%, 18%, 17%, 14%, 11%, 14%	11%, 12%, 16%, 9%, 11%, 11%	9%, 12%, 12%, 11%, 8%, 14%	44%, 39%, 38%, 39%, 47%, 40%

Numbers in bold are statistically higher / lower than average.

○ All ○ Media-engaged ○ Less media-engaged

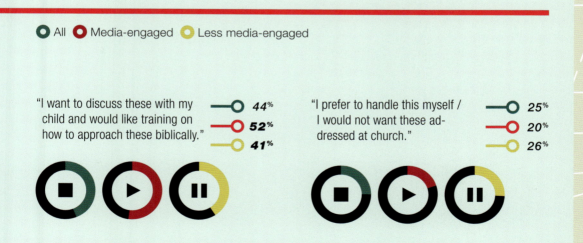

"I want to discuss these with my child and would like training on how to approach these biblically."
- 44%
- 52%
- 41%

"I prefer to handle this myself / I would not want these addressed at church."
- 25%
- 20%
- 26%

Numbers in bold are statistically higher / lower than average.

3 . CHURCH FAMILIES

For engaged Christian parents, church is a family affair. And even though children may be small, they carry big weight when it comes to family decisions about where to worship. **Nearly six in 10 highly engaged Christian parents say children's programming is the *primary* reason they chose their current church (58%).** As we might expect, church-guided parents—who look to church leaders for faith formation guidance—are more likely to highly prioritize the children's ministry when selecting a church home (64% say this is their primary reason for choosing where to attend vs. 52% of self-guided parents).

For churches to attract and retain strong Christian families, children's programming must be a key part of holistic family ministry.

Children's Program Is the Primary Reason for Church Choice

- Strongly agree — 22%
- Somewhat agree — 36%
- Somewhat disagree — 24%
- Strongly disagree — 18%

n=506 U.S. engaged Christian parents with at least one child age 6 to 12, Sept.–Oct. 2018.

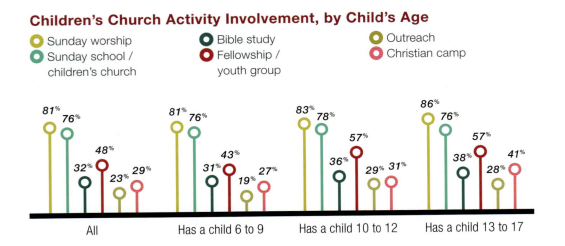

n=506 U.S. engaged Christian parents with at least one child age 6 to 12, Sept.–Oct. 2018.

As any parent can confirm, regular church attendance with a kid can be a challenge. So how often are families making it to church?

In general, more than one might think. Regardless of what region you're in, about three in five engaged Christians' children attend church every week. This is as true in the West and Northeast (generally speaking, more unchurched) as it is in the South.

Attendance at Sunday worship appears quite consistent across age groups, hovering in the 80- to 88-percent range across the span of childhood years. Sunday school attendance trails by only a few percentage points across these years. The dedicated truly are dedicated.

That said, various factors appear to impact the likelihood of a family attending church on a regular basis. As one example, two-thirds of married people's children (64%) attend church every week, compared to half of single parents' kids (51%). **For some, the weeklong work and parenting demands of a typical single parent means less time and energy even for a family activity that's very important to them, such as attending church.** For others, it may be a logistical issue having to do with weekend custody.

In a similar (and often related) vein, household income is also a predictor for how often a family attends. Families with

Churched Level by Household Income
◯ <$30k ◯ $30–$60k ◯ $60–$100k ◯ $100k+

Church engaged: 54%, 56%, 63%, 64%
Miss one Sunday: 39%, 35%, 20%, 22%

n=506 U.S. engaged Christian parents with at least one child age 6 to 12, Sept.–Oct. 2018.

lower household income are more likely than others to miss one Sunday a month. The percentage differences between economic groups for church-engaged are not statistically significant; those who attend *every* week are dedicated, regardless of financial situation. But families who miss a week here and there are more likely to have less income, perhaps due to inconsistent work schedules.

No matter how committed they are, there are days when parents just can't make it to church. It might be easy for ministry leaders to feel, when they see empty seats, that attendance is a low priority for parents—but that's not usually the case. Researchers asked parents two related questions: What prevented them from making it to church, and how often they participated in online services. The good news? **When engaged Christian families miss church, they typically have a good reason.**

About two out of three report that illness (33%) or travel (29%) were the cause of their last absence. Half of young parents ages 24 to 34 say they missed church because someone was sick (52%). Young families, especially, are doing their best to be there. (But sometimes the flu says otherwise!)

Fewer report they were "too tired" (6%) or they "didn't feel like going" (9%). In a noticeable jump, older parents are more willing than younger ones to say they simply "didn't feel like going" (31% vs. 5%). Could this point to disengagement or a diminished value of church in the minds of older parents? (Alternately, some may just be tired!)

Reasons for Missing Church
- Sick — 33%
- Out of town — 29%
- Had an activity — 13%
- Didn't feel like going — 9%
- Too tired — 6%
- Other — 10%

n=506 U.S. engaged Christian parents with at least one child age 6 to 12, Sep.–Oct. 2018.

Parents in the Northeast are more likely to say they skipped church due to an activity compared to parents living in other regions. Given that the Northeast is a highly unchurched region, it seems possible that events are scheduled at times that frequently conflict with church services more often than in other regions.

What about engaging with a service via the internet? Roughly one in three says they "never" watch a church service online (30%). Among the one-quarter of all engaged Christian parents (24%) who watch two or more times per month, doing so is more common among African Americans (45%) and single parents (32% vs. 21% married).

The crux of the matter is this: **Even when they are absent, parents' desire to be with their church family (with kids in tow) is strong—so strong that many "go" to church any way they can.**

Continued on page 59

Frequency: Watch Online?
- 2+ times a month — 24%
- Once a month — 12%
- Once every 2 months — 5%
- Once every 3–4 months — 6%
- Less often — 22%
- Never — 30%

n=506 U.S. engaged Christian parents with at least one child age 6 to 12, Sep.–Oct. 2018.

Stages of Spiritual Development

By Hettie Brittz

Spiritual development is closely tied to moral development phases—how growing children process the ideas of right and wrong, safe and unsafe, good and bad. These are very abstract concepts for a while and only become concrete later in childhood.

From ages 3 to 5 there's a phase of wonder. Kids are very much impressed by the miracles God can do. It's almost a magical phase—where the stories about the miracles of Christ, the plagues or Samson's strength really grab their attention. Kids see God almost like a superhero with incredible powers. During this time, they need to be taught how the wonder points to the inner powers, such as love, that makes God better than any superhero.

The 5-year-old starts getting ready to understand some of that and the 6-year-old, depending on their development and personality, can move onto a next phase that's very, very different. (Six-year-olds are right on "the crack" between the two spiritual developmental phases on either side.)

The years from 6 to 10 are almost ruled by fear. Kids become acutely aware of how real dangers are in the world around them. They become aware of illness. It's the age when parents start telling them, "We're not going to grandma's because she is sick." Parents start talking about death. Children are more exposed, more active out of the house. They see the world a bit more clearly. During this time, one of their primary felt needs is to know, *How can God protect me?* The world has become so much bigger, so they want to know how "big" God is and how his power can help them.

This is a phase when we sometimes think children are too small to deal with difficult truths, so we are tempted to give them a false foundation. This is an extreme example, but something along the lines of, "If you pray Psalm 91 before you go to bed, then the bad guys can't come into the house." We try to give them concrete guarantees of safety, but that undermines faith when people *do* die. Not everybody we pray for gets healed and things don't always go smoothly. In this phase, we need to understand that they could develop a very unhelpful fear of God because of this propensity to be afraid.

Then, from age 11 onward, there is a stronger focus on morality. There is an acute awareness of sin, uncertainty whether they are good enough for God. Usually they want to know what "the rules" are. They regard faith as making the right choices, believing the right things, having the right information and living right. Right, right, right.

This is a wonderful phase for them to be introduced to concepts of grace, forgiveness, confession and the power of the Holy Spirit to enable us to live the Christian life. It's really in this phase they can get their heads around Jesus dying on the cross for us in very meaningful ways. Earlier on it's almost a little too scary and too concrete, and kids who are exposed to the crucifixion of Christ in a very graphic manner before that age often go into extreme guilt about what "they" have done to Christ, personally and individually, unless they are guided carefully through that.

When we as parents demonstrate both God's justice and his forgiveness in consistent ways in that phase from 10 to 12, it is the best spiritual gift we can give our children. ●

(See bio on page 26.)

Guiding Healthier Transitions

By Beth Green

While our kids are being forced to deal with "adult" topics and media at younger ages, there is a bigger story: In our culture, transitions into *real* adulthood are being delayed. Thinking back to my grandparents' generation, young people left school at age 12 or 13 to begin apprenticeships and start functioning as adults. But today, the idea of a preadolescent developmental transition is far more significant, and chronological phases are drawn out.

At age 12 today, a child is not yet a teenager, and certainly not an adult. In some senses they're being given permission to grow up, while in other ways—including emotionally, psychologically and spiritually—they're not being encouraged to mature into the responsibilities of adulthood. Technology may push kids to experience mature ideas, but they lack the support and structure of the healthy expectations of their community to help them transition into the next phase of their lives. ●

(See bio on page 31.)

Church-Engaged Children

For the six in 10 Christian parents who report attending church on a weekly basis, we will see that their high involvement in church is echoed in other domains of family life. These are church-engaged families, and their faithfulness in a worshiping community correlates with other faith-forming activities. (When it comes to activities that are not specific to Christians, church-engaged and less engaged kids' lives look similar.)

For example, children who are most active in church tend to engage with the Bible *outside* of church, to attend church activities other than Sunday worship (such as Bible studies, camps or children's/youth events), and to pray together with their family as well. They are also about *twice* as likely to engage in outreach activities and volunteerism, demonstrating that the level of dedication in this group to the overall mission of the church is not only internally focused, but expresses itself in outward action.

Families who are established in their church are more likely to be church-engaged. They've put down roots. By the same token, they are *less* likely to be at a new church than parents with less-engaged children. (Said differently, among families who are in their first year of attending a church, 60% fall into the "less church-engaged" category and do not attend weekly.)

Perhaps unsurprisingly, three out of five church-engaged parents are very satisfied with their children's spiritual formation thus far (61% vs. 51%). They are also more likely to rely on their church for the faith development of their kids (72% vs. 63%). Less church-engaged parents, by comparison, are more likely to look to extended family as key to their child's faith development (39% vs. 30%).

But while being a church-engaged parent bodes well for many aspects of

Weekly Church Attendance, by Bible Engagement

○ Church-engaged ○ Less church-engaged

n=506 U.S. engaged Christian parents with at least one child age 6 to 12, Sept.–Oct. 2018.

Church Activities (within the Past Year)

○ Church-engaged ○ Less church-engaged

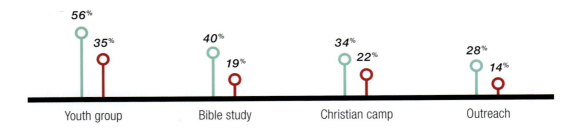

| Youth group | Bible study | Christian camp | Outreach |

Family Activities (within the Past Month)

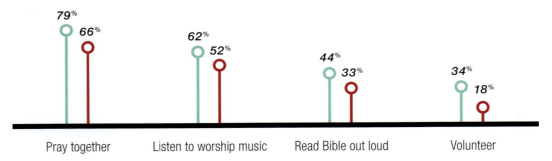

n=506 U.S. engaged Christian parents with at least one child age 6 to 12, Sept.–Oct. 2018.

parenting, there is reason to believe that church-engaged parents tend to have a rosier view of the age their child is exposed to negative material or experiences. These parents are far more likely to say their children are not exposed to sensitive or problematic things until after they're 15 years old (see p. 65). It is easy to speculate that heavy church involvement could somewhat disconnect parents from the realities many kids face—but alternately, church-engaged parents may be more vigilant about what their children encounter outside the house and "in the wild."

Researchers asked engaged Christian parents about their children's engagement with "extracurricular" church activities (such as Christian camps, youth group or

Bible study), while also gauging their level of involvement with more general extracurricular participation.

The picture that emerges shows significant correlation between a family committing to participation in *general* extracurricular activity for their children and their commitment to extracurricular *church* activities. In other words, families already doing quite a bit are likely to do more, while children who aren't involved as often in general extracurricular activity are less likely to get involved in church-specific activities (see p. 66). Just one example? Kids or youth with high extracurricular commitments are nearly *twice* as likely to be involved in a church Bible study as kids who have fewer extracurricular commitments.

Overcommitment of a child's time is a real issue today, and these numbers should not be used to pressure more involvement from families who have little margin. But there appears to be a *type* of family whose high level of engagement encompasses both Christian and secular

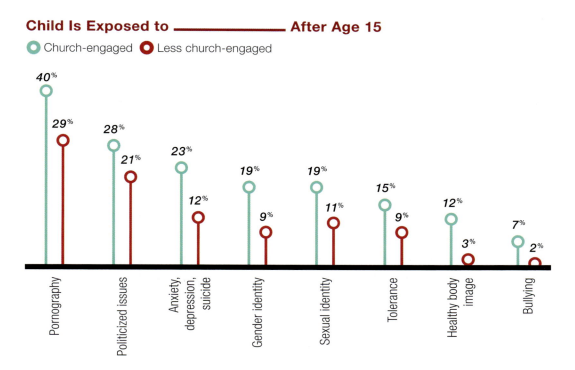

Child Is Exposed to ———————— After Age 15

○ Church-engaged ○ Less church-engaged

- Pornography: 40% / 29%
- Politicized issues: 28% / 21%
- Anxiety, depression, suicide: 23% / 12%
- Gender identity: 19% / 9%
- Sexual identity: 19% / 11%
- Tolerance: 15% / 9%
- Healthy body image: 12% / 3%
- Bullying: 7% / 2%

n=506 U.S. engaged Christian parents with at least one child age 6 to 12, Sep.–Oct. 2018.

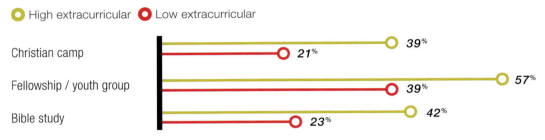

Children's Involvement in Church Activities

○ High extracurricular ○ Low extracurricular

Christian camp: 21% / 39%
Fellowship / youth group: 39% / 57%
Bible study: 23% / 42%

n=506 U.S. engaged Christian parents with at least one child age 6 to 12, Sept.–Oct. 2018.

opportunities for involvement. When there is a healthy balance, church leaders should not feel that their ministry is "just one more thing" for busy families. Church activities can be part of a vibrant and thriving schedule for a developing child— and already *are* for many families.

Parents & Kids in Spiritual Conversation

Parenting is perhaps the greatest imaginable opportunity for long-term conversation. No other life role offers such an intimate and constant opportunity to engage questions and develop ongoing dialog. Just ask a committed parent, and they will likely have many stories of conversations with their kid, moments that were meaningful, challenging, satisfying, hilariously awkward—or all of the above.

Conversations about spirituality tend to start young. "Who made the world?" "Does God love me?" "Why do bad things happen?" From early on, these questions invite parents to consider their own faith and test their skill at putting deep concepts into child-friendly formats.

How prepared do parents feel to be guides in spiritual conversations with their kids? It varies, but in general parents are confident. **When asked how well their church has equipped them to have faith-focused conversations with their child, nearly half report feeling "extremely well" equipped (46%).** An additional two in five say "very well" (39%). In fact, only 2 percent of parents report feeling completely out of their depth.

One interesting dynamic is that parents with less education tend to say they

Parents Feeling Equipped for Spiritual Conversations

- Extremely well — 46%
- Very well — 39%
- Somewhat well — 12%
- Not at all — 2%

Parents Feeling Equipped, by Education Level

	Extremely well	Very well	Somewhat well	Not at all
High school or less	58%	36%	2%	4%
Some college or trade school	47%	32%	18%	3%
College graduate or more	38%	48%	12%	1%

n=506 U.S. engaged Christian parents with at least one child age 6 to 12, Sept.–Oct. 2018.

feel better equipped to have spiritual conversations than those with more education. One possible reason might be that those with less education have different or simpler ideas of what a spiritual conversation with their kids should look like. Or perhaps their perception of faith is simpler—they do not feel the need to caveat for possible future intellectual barriers to faith in later adolescence or through exposure to new ideas during the college experience. Whatever the case, better-educated parents may need more encouragement and guidance from ministry leaders.

Given their greater dependence on their church for guidance (as we saw in chapter 1), it's not surprising that parents of media-engaged children say they find it difficult to discuss faith-focused topics with their children. This is less often the case among less media-engaged families.

What is holding them back from taking initiative with their kids to lead these conversations? Church leaders may be able to drill down here to uncover if parents' reluctance comes from a lack of resourcing or weakness in family relationships. In either case, **there is a strategic opportunity for church leaders to lean into an urgent (if quiet) need among media-engaged families in their faith community.**

Waxing & Waning Interest in Church

For any of us—kids included—there can be an ebb and flow in our desire to engage in church life. But the story of fluctuating interest over the course of childhood has interesting implications for how church fits into the larger story of a young person's spiritual life.

For all young people—those Barna classifies as church-engaged and those who are less engaged—interest often declines a bit as a child enters the middle teenage years. But a sharp disparity emerges when comparing these two groups year over year. In the long run, less church-engaged teens are more likely than those who attend every Sunday to lose interest in church.

Among church-engaged young people, interest in attending church tends to

Continued on page 67

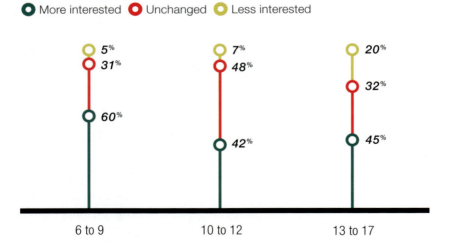

Changing Interest in Church Attendance, by Child's Age

● More interested ● Unchanged ● Less interested

	6 to 9	10 to 12	13 to 17
Less interested	5%	7%	20%
Unchanged	31%	48%	32%
More interested	60%	42%	45%

n=506 U.S. engaged Christian parents with at least one child age 6 to 12, Sept.–Oct. 2018.

The Gift of a Parent's Presence
By Bryan Cheney

The research into kids retaining their faith as they grow points toward the need for family warmth. The families that have a high "stickiness" factor aren't just those who read the Bible every night, but those who simply enjoy each other's company and have fun together.

In understanding that, we've decided that one of the best things we can do for families is model the importance of this practice and provide them with opportunities to be together. When we plan an event we don't just say, "Here's an event to entertain your kids. Drop them off and we'll teach them about the Bible." I call that a "carwash mentality." Instead, our mentality is, "Here's an event that will help your whole family. It's an example of something you could do regularly to learn and spend time together and build your relationship. We want to partner with your family."

If our families can say, "One of the best things we ever did as a family is come to church regularly," we feel like we're winning.

(See bio on page 30.)

Primary Shapers of Belief
By Janelle Schroy

Church typically gets a small slice of time in a child's life, often just an hour and a half once a week. This means parents have far more time and opportunity for influence—as well as more responsibility to shape the character of their child—than a church does.

Parents need to think of themselves as primary shapers of their children's belief structures. But they also need to know they are not alone. Church leaders need to help parents understand the importance of deepening their relationships through shared experiences. No one else knows and understands a child the way a parent does—not a youth pastor, not a children's minister, not a teacher. In fact, I like to use the word "mentor" or "guide" to describe a parent who guides their child in the process of discovering their belief structure.

This powerful parental influence happens through time spent together. I remember reading a Harvard study that discovered the number one predictor of a child's future happiness was the quality of their closest relationships when they were young. And of course, quality relationships come through time spent together.

Churches might be tempted to think that they just need to give parents another app or video or webinar to help them be better parents. But it's about *time*. Another study found that the average amount of quality time parents spent with kids every day is only 34 minutes. Time spent well has been lost in our culture. How can the church help reverse this? How can we creatively respond to gather kids and parents into shared experiences, instead of constantly separating them when they walk into church?

I'm on this parenting journey myself, and I've found the best possible thing I can do with my seven-year-old daughter is to go on a date at a coffee shop with her every week. We have a shared mother-daughter journal with prompts in it that we pass back and forth. She will write things to me that she doesn't say in person or will ask questions she's too embarrassed to ask out loud.

I can talk at her all day long, and send her to school and to workshops, but at the end of the day the quality of our relationship depends on my time spent with her. My personal, physical, undivided presence—apart from technology—is the best gift I can give. ●

JANELLE SCHROY *is the visionary, product creator and key spokewoman for Adventure Clubs, which she designed out of her desire to create a meaningful life with her family. She is married to her Adventure Clubs co-founder, Jedd Schroy, and they have four daughters.*

decline between the ages of 10 and 12, then remain fairly consistent through the high school years.

Compare that to less church-engaged young people. They are significantly more likely to be disinterested in church at a younger age (6 to 9), with a sharp spike in that disinterest when they are 12 to 13. Once they reach high school, disinterest leaps—about three in 10 becoming disinterested in church, compared to roughly one in seven church-engaged youth.

In short, consistency matters. **Engagement in a community of faith is a slow cooker, not a microwave.** Many of the "persistence benefits" of consistent

Declining Interest by Church Engagement
○ All ○ Church-engaged ○ Less church-engaged

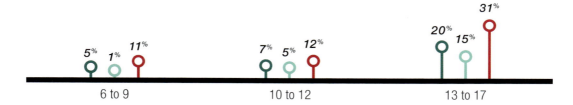

Increasing Interest by Church Engagement
○ All ○ Church-engaged ○ Less church-engaged

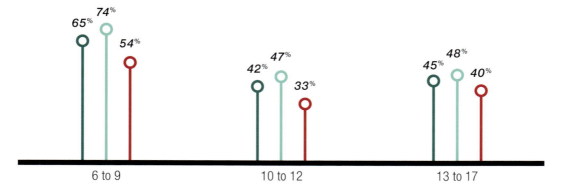

n=506 U.S. engaged Christian parents with at least one child age 6 to 12, Sept.–Oct. 2018.

Three Key Trends Affecting Kids Today

By Beth McCauley

1. Kids today lack persistence.
They avoid struggles and challenges, and give up easily. They become frustrated when they can't quickly get an answer from adults. We call this a lack of "grit." In my experience, we're seeing fewer children work hard, endure struggles, accept failure, and get up to try again. One contributing factor may be that increasingly parents seem to resolve challenges for their children. Often, parents truly want to do what's right for their child, but that desire results in them resolving the situation themselves instead of allowing their child to struggle to a resolution.

2. Children today need intentional physical activity to maintain focus.
This could certainly be related to the fact that children aren't getting enough activity outside of the school day because they're spending more time inside using technology. A decade or so ago, schools pulled back from physical church involvement aren't truly felt until a young person's high school experience is well underway. While there are a host of reasons a young person might lose interest in church, **the data clearly show that being part of a family that is regular in church attendance plays a part in keeping high schoolers engaged in their congregation.**

Most parents are willing guides for their child's spiritual development, and a majority of them say their church plays a vital role in helping them help their child navigate the spiritual journeys of youth and childhood. Church matters—deeply—as part of the whole picture of childhood faith formation.

Regular church attendance in childhood plays an important role in young people's long-range faith picture. As parents and church leaders consider together how best to nurture the personhood and faith of younger Christians, one thing is vital to remember: We are all in this together, and each guide in a child's life is dynamically important for their faith and development.

education, believing they needed to focus on core subjects and academics, and there wasn't time for physical education. But we're now understanding that we have to up the level of movement throughout the day in order to engage them. Whatever the reason, it's impacting their cognitive skills and ability to focus—they need to move to create space for learning.

3. Technology affects children's emotional engagement.

I've seen this in schools where children are given iPads and take surveys that ask how they feel by allowing them to click on happy or sad faces. If we continue to do that, we're diminishing their ability to put emotions into words. The ability to express yourself verbally is essential for success in life, but that ability can be stifled by technology. One way we can develop this is by giving children opportunities and space at home and at school to express their emotions without being criticized or stifled—and giving them a full palette of language to express themselves. (I've also seen a tendency for adults to step in and provide responses for children instead of allowing them to struggle and practice responding to difficult situations emotionally. This goes back to the need for parents and educators to help children develop grit.) ●

BETH McCAULEY *has been an educator for more than 30 years.*

Guided by the Spirit & the Word

Passing resilient faith on to children is less likely to happen by default or by accident in this increasingly complex and accelerated culture. This study makes clear that engaged Christian parents don't expect this calling to be easy, but also that they do consider it a *calling*—a sacred, God-ordained assignment in service to his expansive Kingdom mission.

Making and growing young disciples is *not* easy, as plenty of previous Barna research shows, but churches and parents can partner to more effectively guide kids along the way. **Children's ministries play an enormous role in the lives of Christian families.** Remember, a majority of parents says their church's program for kids is the primary reason they chose their fellowship. Nearly half say they rely most on their church, rather than themselves, as the key spiritual influence in their child's life. A majority wants help with teaching their kids about difficult social issues, and many are actively looking for resources that can help them with their child's spiritual formation.

And that's all *before* we get to the issues of media, entertainment and technology!

Imagine how powerful this partnership could be if ministry leaders and parents shift their focus from simply limiting screen time to releasing disciples. Rather than "How much is too much?" we could wrestle with bigger questions:

- How can we set youth up for healthy online habits—not just avoiding harmful content, but initiating and engaging in conversations for spiritual growth and the common good?
- What do Christian virtues or disciplines look like in digital spaces?
- What are some opportunities for digital natives to live out their Christian faith that didn't exist for older generations?
- How do we connect kids with wise guides to help them navigate the increasing complexities of childhood?
- How can new technology interface with the timeless Christian message?
- How can leaders listen to emerging generations for input and ideas regarding what needs they feel around digital life and habits?
- How can we give the Bible its proper place in the lives of young Jesus followers?

Christian parents are not the only parents grappling with the role of media in their children's lives. While highly engaged Christians are likely to feel the dilemmas and dangers of tech and media saturation more keenly than many others, they are certainly not the only parents who do. People of other faiths, the "spiritual but not religious," and even atheist and agnostic neighbors are all asking hard questions. How do we raise children well in this transitional era in history?

Answering that question well is an opportunity for Christians to serve and lead within the broader culture. **The shared challenge of parenting in this context presents us with a chance to meet and listen to and share with our non-Christian neighbors**—not just in our churches but in our living rooms, schools, community centers and even our social media feeds.

As Spirit-led parents and their church ministry partners guide children to put tech in its proper place in their God-honoring lives, the countercultural Kingdom will come a little bit more on earth as in heaven. The *goodness* of Christianity for individuals, families and communities will be as evident as its truth.

How can ministry leaders equip Christian parents for everyday evangelism?

Because in the end, evangelism is exactly what we're doing when we pass faith on to the next generation.

We want our children's relationships with media and devices to be healthy and life-giving. We want young people to invest in and wisely lead the Church's future.

And most of all, we want our kids to inherit a deep love for and knowledge of God's Word, to experience Jesus for themselves and to allow his Spirit to be their Guide.

> When the Spirit of truth comes, he will guide you into all truth.
> *(John 16:13)*

A. Notes

1. Common Sense Media, "The Common Sense Census: Media Use by Tweens and Teens," p.19. https://www.commonsensemedia.org/sites/default/files/uploads/research/census_researchreport.pdf (accessed July 2019).

2. Karen Zraik, "Teenagers Say Depression and Anxiety Are Major Issues Among Their Peers," *The New York Times,* February 20, 2019. https://www.nytimes.com/2019/02/20/health/teenage-depression-statistics.html.

3. Hayley Tsukayama, "Teens Spend Nearly Nine Hours Every Day Consuming Media," *The Washington Post*, Nov. 3, 2015. https://www.washingtonpost.com/news/the-switch/wp/2015/11/03/teens-spend-nearly-nine-hours-every-day-con

4. American Psychological Association, "Age of First Exposure to Pornography Shapes Men's Attitudes Toward Women," research presented to the 125th Convention of the APA, August 3, 2017.

B. Methodology

This study began with qualitative interviews of toy developers, children's ministry leaders, educators, child development specialists and technology professionals. These interviews were conducted in the fall of 2018 and used a flexible script to explore respondents' experiences in their specific fields.

A set of quantitative online surveys was subsequently conducted September 17 to October 18, 2018, using an online panel. The sample included 508 self-identified U.S. Christian parents of children ages 6 to 12 who are engaged in their Christian faith. Barna defines "engaged" as follows: They have attended a Christian church service within the past month (other than for a holiday or a special event); they strongly agree that the Bible is the inspired Word of God and contains truth about the world; they strongly agree that they believe Jesus Christ was crucified and raised from the dead to conquer sin and death; they strongly agree that they have made a personal commitment to Jesus Christ that is still important in their life today; and they strongly agree that they desire to pass faith on to their child.

The margin of error for this sample is +/- 4.2 percentage points at the 95% confidence level.

All research that seeks to capture the dynamics of a population has inherent limitations, but is useful to observe patterns and differences that reveal insights about the surveyed group. Online panels are a collection of people who have pre-agreed to take surveys for compensation, which may represent some motivational biases, so our surveys include quality control measures to ensure respondents are providing truthful and thoughtful answers to questions.

When Barna samples from panels, respondents are invited from a randomly selected group of people matching the demographics of the U.S. population for maximum representation. For this study, researchers set quotas to obtain a minimum readable sample by a variety of demographic factors and weighted the data by region, gender, ethnicity and education to reflect their natural presence in the U.S. population (using U.S. Census Bureau and Bureau of Labor Statistics data for comparison). More specifically, we weighted the data to reflect those U.S. adults who have Generation Z children.

Partly by nature of using an online panel, these respondents are slightly more educated and higher earning than the average American. Also, due to the natural makeup of the practicing Christian population, the proportion of black adults is greater than Hispanic adults when compared to the general U.S. population.

ACKNOWLEDGEMENTS

Barna Group wishes to thank our partners at OneHope, especially the research team led by Dr. Tena Stone, who co-labored with us to conduct the parent and expert interviews: Christine E. Schaeffer, Ph.D., Dave Plate, Kathie Coenen, Madison Chastain and Patricia Savage. Thank you for your dedication, drive and passion!

The research team for *Guiding Children* is Brooke Hempell, Savannah Kimberlin, Pam Jacob and Aly Hawkins. Under the editorial direction of Roxanne Stone, Aly Hawkins and Paul Pastor created this report. David Kinnaman and Brooke Hempell contributed additional analysis and insights. Doug Brown edited the manuscript. Roxanne Stone and Aly Hawkins developed the data visualizations, which were, along with the report, designed by Annette Allen. Chaz Russo designed the cover. Brenda Usery managed production with project management assistance from Jennifer Hamel and Mallory Holt.

The *Guiding Children* team wishes to thank our Barna colleagues Amy Brands, Cory Maxwell-Coghlan, Daniel Copeland, Aidan Dunn, Janet Eason, Traci Hochmuth, Joe Jensen, Steve McBeth, Susan Mettes, Rhesa Storms, Jess Villa, Todd White and Alyce Youngblood.

BARNA GROUP is a research firm dedicated to providing actionable insights on faith and culture, with a particular focus on the Christian church. In its 35-year history, Barna has conducted more than one million interviews in the course of hundreds of studies, and has become a go-to source for organizations that want to better understand a complex and changing world from a faith perspective.

Barna's clients and partners include a broad range of academic institutions, churches, nonprofits and businesses, such as Alpha, the Templeton Foundation, Fuller Seminary, the Bill and Melinda Gates Foundation, Maclellan Foundation, DreamWorks Animation, Focus Features, Habitat for Humanity, The Navigators, NBC-Universal, the ONE Campaign, Paramount Pictures, the Salvation Army, Walden Media, Sony and World Vision. The firm's studies are frequently quoted by major media outlets such as *The Economist*, BBC, CNN, *USA Today*, the *Wall Street Journal*, Fox News, Huffington Post, *The New York Times* and the *Los Angeles Times*.

www.Barna.com

ONEHOPE is a global organization resourcing partners and churches to present a Scripture-rich Gospel message to children and youth in a way they can understand. In the past three decades, we have helped reach more than 1.5 billion children and youth worldwide with the Gospel. This year alone, we have an audacious goal of reaching 123 million more with a life-changing message of purpose and hope. To find out more about what we do, where we work and who we partner with, visit us online.

www.OneHope.net

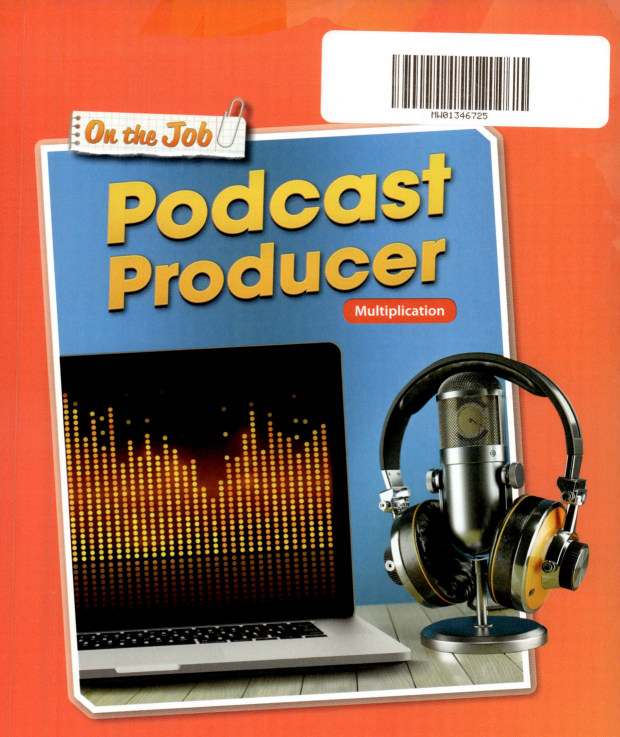

On the Job

Podcast Producer

Multiplication

Georgia Beth

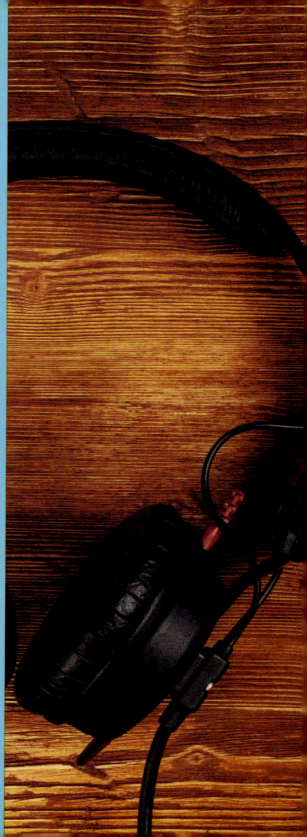

Consultants

Michele Ogden, Ed.D
Principal
Irvine Unified School District

Colleen Pollitt, M.A.Ed.
Math Support Teacher
Howard County Public Schools

Publishing Credits

Rachelle Cracchiolo, M.S.Ed., *Publisher*
Conni Medina, M.A.Ed., *Managing Editor*
Dona Herweck Rice, *Series Developer*
Emily R. Smith, M.A.Ed., *Series Developer*
Diana Kenney, M.A.Ed., NBCT, *Content Director*
Stacy Monsman, M.A., *Editor*
Kevin Panter, *Graphic Designer*

Image Credits: p. 15 Illustration by Timothy J. Bradley; all other images from iStock and/or Shutterstock.

Library of Congress Cataloging-in-Publication Data

Names: Beth, Georgia, author.
Title: Podcast producer / Georgia Beth.
Description: Huntington Beach, CA : Teacher Created Materials, Inc., [2018] | Series: On the job | Includes index.
Identifiers: LCCN 2017011831 (print) | LCCN 2017014473 (ebook) | ISBN 9781480759312 (eBook) | ISBN 9781425855499 (pbk.)
Subjects: LCSH: Podcasting--Juvenile literature. | Webometrics--Juvenile literature.
Classification: LCC TK5105.887 (ebook) | LCC TK5105.887 .B48 2018 (print) | DDC 791.44/6--dc23
LC record available at https://lccn.loc.gov/2017011831

Teacher Created Materials

5301 Oceanus Drive
Huntington Beach, CA 92649-1030
http://www.tcmpub.com

ISBN 978-1-4258-5549-9
© 2018 Teacher Created Materials, Inc.

Table of Contents

Seen, Not Heard 4

Tech Talk 6

Money Matters 10

Getting Creative 14

Being Seen 21

Building a Following 26

Problem Solving 28

Glossary 30

Index 31

Answer Key 32

This is a work of fiction. Names, characters, businesses, places, events, and incidents are either the products of the author's imagination or used in a fictitious manner. Any resemblance to actual persons, living or dead, or actual events is purely coincidental.

Seen, Not Heard

Ping! Neeka smiles at the sound of her post going live. She knows her readers will love getting an exclusive look at her new food capsule idea. Neeka hopes this post is as popular as "Why Space Travel in Movies Is Unrealistic."

But the next day when Neeka checks her **analytics**, she sighs. Her blog only has 9,973 visitors. Neeka reminds herself that's almost 10,000 if she rounds. But Piper's blog gets about 100,000 hits every day. Even if the actual number is 89,763, it's still a lot—10 times more, in fact! Neeka decides she needs to up her game.

Neeka thinks of ways to get more visitors to her blog.

Neeka starts scribbling in her notebook. She has so many ideas; it's hard to make a plan. She scrolls through old texts from Piper.

Neeka leans back from her laptop. It's clear that Piper loves podcasts. In fact, all of their friends love podcasts, especially Jiro. He said podcasts are the new thing. Neeka grins. She decides it's time to start a podcast about sci-fi!

Neeka grabs her phone to text Piper.

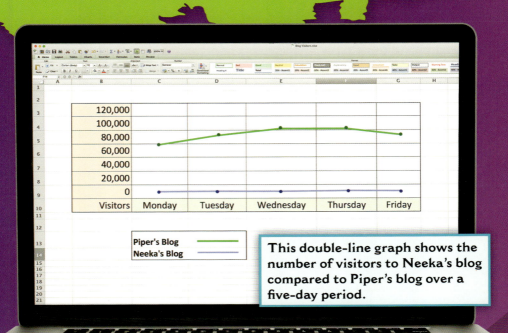

This double-line graph shows the number of visitors to Neeka's blog compared to Piper's blog over a five-day period.

Tech Talk

Neeka decides the first thing she needs to do is listen to a podcast about how to start a podcast! With a giggle, Neeka grabs her **bullet journal**. She starts making a list of questions and **resources**. She writes anything and everything she can think of about podcasts. She fills several pages with notes.

When the list starts becoming too long, Neeka takes a break from writing. She decides to do some more research. As she searches through a list of microphone options, she can't help but laugh at the silly names. She eyes a microphone called *Super Xtreme Mic*, and wonders why they can't use normal names.

Neeka knows she needs several items to begin. First, she'll need a professional microphone and headphones. She'll also need recording software. She worries that this could get pricey. Neeka considers buying some of her pieces used. But, she can't help daydreaming about talking into a giant microphone. After all, she has to splurge somewhere, right?

Neeka meets Piper for lunch to discuss business ideas.

The next day, Neeka meets Piper for their usual business lunch—sitting outside, eating something delicious, and figuring out how to rule the world. That's really all Neeka needs for it to be a good day.

"So you're really going to do this?" Piper asks.

"I'm not *just* going to do this. I'm going to do it the right way. I want to be a podcasting ninja," Neeka replies.

"How are you going to record everything?"

"I just got a new microphone, and I'm going to sync up with my guests through video messaging. Easy."

LET'S EXPLORE MATH

Neeka's podcast is 14 megabytes of data. How many megabytes will Neeka produce if she develops 52 shows per year? Complete the area model and equations to solve the problem.

	50	+	2
10	$10 \times 50 =$ ____		$10 \times 2 =$ ____
+			
4	$4 \times 50 =$ ____		$4 \times 2 =$ ____

"What about editing and uploading?"

"My **Virtual Assistant (VA)** is going to handle that. She already takes care of my social media posts. This is just going to be another thing on her weekly to-do list. She's even going to **index** the episodes, so they'll be easy to find online."

"You're totally going to be the next big thing!"

"It's going to be Neeka Public Radio," she says with a wink.

Neeka's Virtual Assistant (VA)

Money Matters

Neeka is getting excited about her new podcast. But, her inner accountant isn't so sure. Neeka has built a business selling ads on her blog. She is starting a podcast to increase her visibility and build her business. But will all this work actually pay off? She doesn't want to spend all of her time creating podcasts and not getting more visitors to her blog. She needs more eyeballs on her ads.

Neeka tightens her ponytail and opens a **spreadsheet**. It's prep time. She starts by making a list of each task required to create a podcast. Neeka has been able to make $100 per hour with her blog, and she wants to do the same with her podcast.

Neeka multiplies all the hours spent by how much she wants to earn. If she can earn $900 per show, then all the work is worth it. Then again, $1,000 per show would be even better. She scribbles her goal on her whiteboard and gives it a hard squint. She knows that once that goal goes on the wall, she will be dedicated to making it happen.

Neeka types a list of tasks.

Neeka researches sponsors for her podcast.

Neeka quickly considers getting **sponsors**. She can see pros and cons. She finally decides sponsors will be the best way to make money with her podcast. She can get 10 sponsors and charge them $100 for each mention. But, that will mean taking a lot of breaks. *Maybe*, she thinks, *four sponsors is more reasonable*. Then, she can charge them $250 per mention. She wants to make the cost of producing a podcast worth it!

LET'S EXPLORE MATH

Cartoon Patrol is bidding on Neeka's ads. It's willing to pay $75 per mention. If Cartoon Patrol buys 12 mentions per year, how much money will Neeka make? Complete the strategy shown using your understanding of place value.

12 × 75

(____ × ____) = 7 0 0
(____ × ____) = 1 4 0
(____ × ____) =   5 0
(____ × ____) =   1 0

700 + 140 + 50 + 10 = ☐

Neeka starts making a list of brands that sponsor her favorite podcasts. Her first choice is Sci-Fi Swag. They sell the newest science fiction stuff, from T-shirts to mugs. There's also PodGear. They sell microphones and other items. Both are good options. But will her listeners like them as much as she does? Her blog posts with practical tips are always the most popular. Neeka needs a sponsor that is fun and helpful. She finally decides on Cartoon Patrol. Cartoon Patrol's fun ads about the newest television shows will be enjoyable for her listeners, instead of a boring 30 seconds.

Getting Creative

Neeka is ready to focus on content. She grabs every marker she can find and settles in. Every episode will be about science fiction, but there are already lots of podcasts about the subject. If she wants to stand out, Neeka knows she needs to find her **niche**. She flips through *Sci-Fi Weekly* and scrolls through social media. Neeka wants to make something that inspires people to think outside the box.

Listening to music always helps her feel more creative. She lies on her bed, staring at the poster on her wall. The poster shows a swamp creature chasing humans. *Swamp People* is written across the top in creepy lettering. *I wonder what planet swamp people came from. I wonder what it was like,* Neeka muses. *Wait! That can be an idea for a podcast!* Neeka smiles as she thinks about the fun research she can do on swamp people.

Neeka sprawls out on the floor with her notebook. She writes *Private Eye on Sci-Fi* in big letters. She finally knows the name of her podcast!

Neeka writes her first podcast about swamp people.

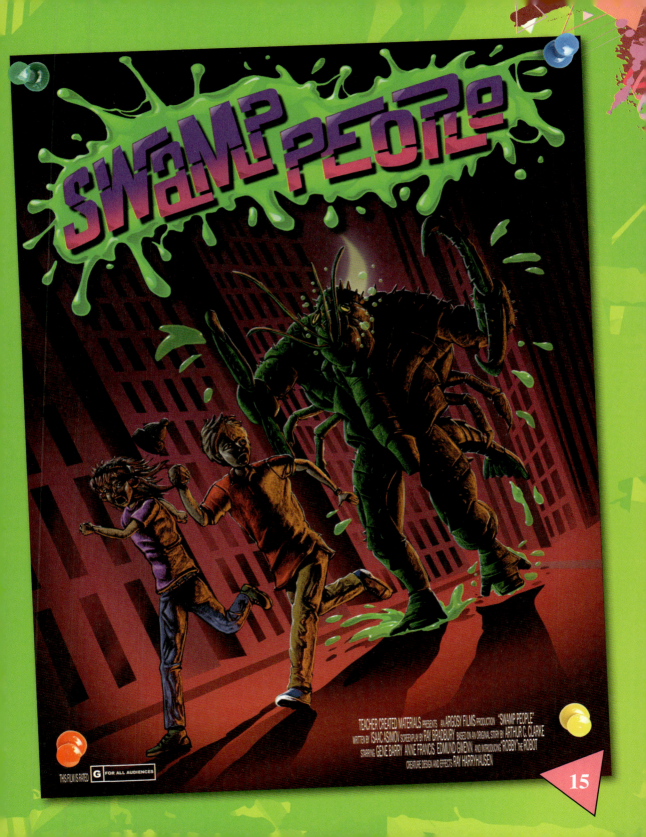

Neeka sketches ideas for the logo of her podcast.

Now that Neeka knows the name of her first episode, she needs to iron out some of the details. She wants each show to be a half-hour long. That is the perfect format for listeners to enjoy on the way to school or while doing chores. Neeka brainstorms a list of topics. Art, music, books, television shows, movies, and news articles can all inspire episodes.

Next, Neeka decides to listen to music while she works. But not just any music will do. Neeka searches for the perfect theme song. She wants something happy. She wants a song that reminds her of futuristic possibilities. As she listens to samples, she begins to sketch a logo. In her spreadsheet, she takes notes on the cost of licensing music and hiring a designer to create a final logo.

After that, she starts scrolling through different podcast categories. It is difficult to choose. Does she want to list her podcast under Science? Neeka doesn't think it's a perfect fit. Maybe it will be more popular under Comic Books? It definitely doesn't belong in News and Politics. Then, she has an idea. She looks at other sci-fi podcasts. *SciLife* has its show listed under Film and Television. *If it's good enough for SciLife, it's good enough for me*! she thinks.

Neeka wants to use her blog know-how to make her podcast successful. She knows readers like the **variety** and **consistency** of her blog. She sorts her blog posts under five headings: Television, Movies, News, Space Travel, and Books. Neeka opens her calendar. Here, she keeps track of her blog topics and when she needs to post them.

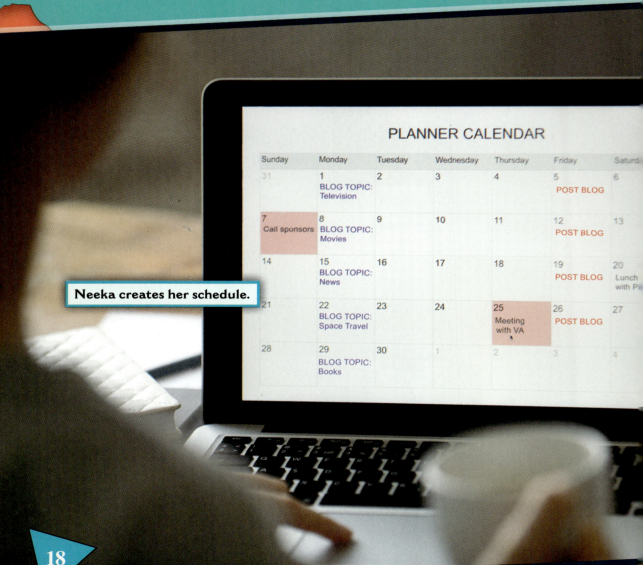

Neeka creates her schedule.

As Neeka brainstorms topics for her podcast, she also thinks about ways to use her podcast to send people to her blog. She wants to tie her blog and podcast together, so more people might visit both. Neeka decides to use the same categories for her podcast. She considers a range of topics for her show. Books or movies can inspire ideas for some episodes. News articles about scientific advancements can spark ideas, too. There can be shows that celebrate classic sci-fi ideas. Anything from space travel, to robots, to life on other planets can be included in a show. *There's always room for fun surprises, too!* Neeka thinks. She hums as she adds deadlines to her calendar. Now, she will know when to post each topic, and she can budget her time.

LET'S EXPLORE MATH

Neeka has some big podcast dreams. But, how big is big?

1. How many episodes will Neeka create if she posts once a week for a year?
2. If each episode is 30 minutes long, how many minutes will she have produced in a year?

Neeka meets with Piper to discuss the progress she has made with her podcast.

Being Seen

At their next business lunch, Neeka gives Piper the rundown. "I'm trying to be really smart about this. I've been looking at all the costs for equipment, training, design, and the VA. I've got it all in my handy spreadsheet."

"That's awesome!" Piper agrees. "Now that you've done some research, how long do you think it's actually going to take to produce each show?"

"Recording will probably take an hour, while editing might take two hours," Neeka replies.

Piper nods, thinking. "How are you going to make sure people know about your show and listen to it?" she asks.

"I've got that covered, too." Neeka closes her eyes, reviewing the invisible spreadsheet she carries in her head these days. "Creating posts for social media and recording interviews will take an hour. Plus, I'll schedule posts, and I can pin links to my website. And, people can read my newsletter to know more about every show, too."

"Hey, I don't know if you would be interested," Piper says shyly. "But I would love to write about *Private Eye on Sci-Fi* on my blog."

"Seriously? That would be amazing!" Neeka nearly topples the table as she leaps up to hug Piper.

"Of course!" Piper gives her a hug. "Just make sure you make time to reply to all of the comments. My readers gush like you wouldn't believe!"

Neeka goes back to business mode, quickly setting a reminder on her phone to update the spreadsheet. "I want my audience—and yours—to feel like I'm their friend."

"That means you'll need to reply to their comments every day, and don't forget emails!"

"You are being so helpful. I'll have to treat you to lunch."

"I'm not going to object," Piper says with a smile.

"You are a great friend!" Neeka laughs.

"Well, you're an **entrepreneurial** (on-truh-pruh-NUR-E-ul) genius!" says Piper.

Back at home, Neeka runs through the numbers for the millionth time. Producing each show will require time and money, but by charging $250 per sponsor, she hopes to do better than break even. Neeka thinks she might even have extra money to score some great guests. She plans to thank them with chocolates, gift cards, and snazzy notebooks. She starts making a list of people to interview.

LET'S EXPLORE MATH

Neeka prepares gift bags for her 15 guests. Each bag includes 12 chocolates, a notebook, a gift card, and a key chain in the guest's favorite color.

1. How many chocolates does Neeka need to buy for her guests? Explain your strategy for finding the solution.

2. If each gift card costs $25, how much will she spend? Show your thinking.

More people begin to visit Neeka's blog and podcast.

Neeka makes her final budget, and the numbers look promising. If she turns a **profit**, she can pour that money back into her blog or podcast. Or, she can treat Piper to more business lunches!

That's not what this is about, Neeka reminds herself as she shakes herself out of a ten-course-lunch daydream. *I started this to get more eyes on my blog. This won't be a success until I build an audience. I need my listeners to read my blog. That's where the real ad money is located.*

Neeka pulls up an article from her research. "People listen to podcasts the way they used to read blogs. Today, five times as many people listen to podcasts as read blogs." *So, if five times as many people listen to my podcast as visit my blog, how many is that?* Neeka checks her analytics. Her latest blog post has 8,765 views. So, five times that is about 45,000 listeners. Neeka smiles, happy with the number. She thinks this podcast might be just what she needs to take her business to the next level.

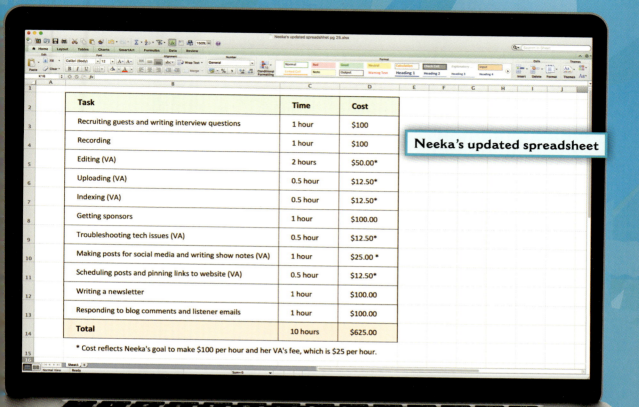

Neeka's updated spreadsheet

Task	Time	Cost
Recruiting guests and writing interview questions	1 hour	$100
Recording	1 hour	$100
Editing (VA)	2 hours	$50.00*
Uploading (VA)	0.5 hour	$12.50*
Indexing (VA)	0.5 hour	$12.50*
Getting sponsors	1 hour	$100.00
Troubleshooting tech issues (VA)	0.5 hour	$12.50*
Making posts for social media and writing show notes (VA)	1 hour	$25.00*
Scheduling posts and pinning links to website (VA)	0.5 hour	$12.50*
Writing a newsletter	1 hour	$100.00
Responding to blog comments and listener emails	1 hour	$100.00
Total	10 hours	$625.00

* Cost reflects Neeka's goal to make $100 per hour and her VA's fee, which is $25 per hour.

LET'S EXPLORE MATH

Neeka is updating her cost spreadsheet. She wants to make $1,000 in revenue per episode. If she charges each sponsor $250, how many sponsors will she need per episode?

1. Write a multiplication equation to represent this situation. Use □ for the unknown factor.
2. If it costs her $625 to make each episode, how much profit will she make per episode?

Building a Following

"Welcome to *Private Eye on Sci-Fi*. From deep space to here on Earth, I explore anything and everything sci-fi. Today, I'll be interviewing Paul Kwon. Or, as you may know him, Jason from the new television series *Intergalactic Expedition*. He can give us the inside scoop about life behind the camera. We're so glad to have you with us."

Neeka interviews Paul Kwon.

Neeka pauses her recording and plays it back to make sure her opening sounds clear. It has been six months since the launch of her podcast. With 26,000 downloads, her latest episode has a bigger audience than she dared to dream. Plus, her blog is growing faster than ever. She is on track to have 10 times as many visitors as when she started the podcast. The best part is hearing how her show inspires her listeners. Seeing their positive comments is better than any analytic report.

Neeka doesn't know what her next project will be. But, she knows she will rise to the challenge. She is hungry for more. She is also hungry for lunch.

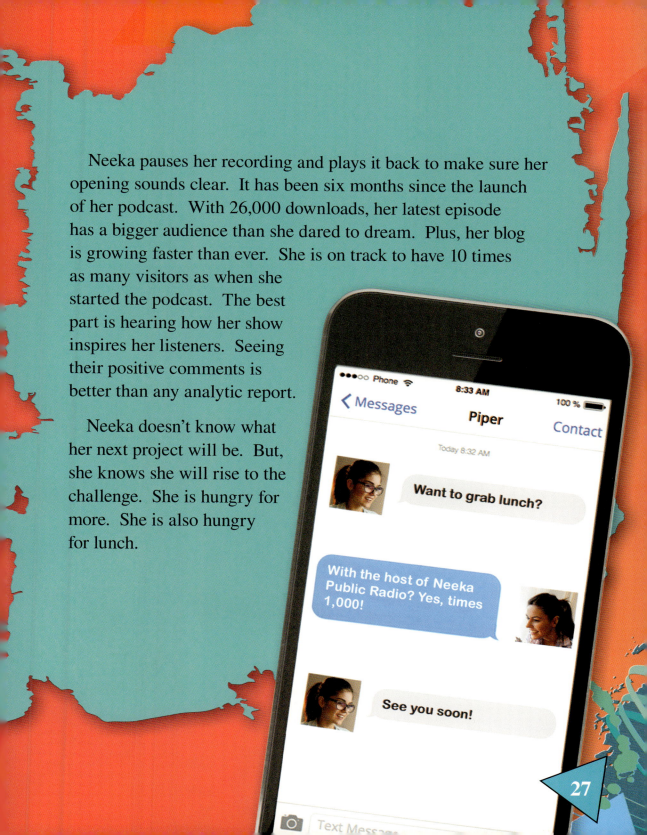

Problem Solving

Now it's your turn to launch a podcast. Choose a topic you know well and that you think listeners will like. Choose a name for your show. Next, draw a logo. Then, answer the questions.

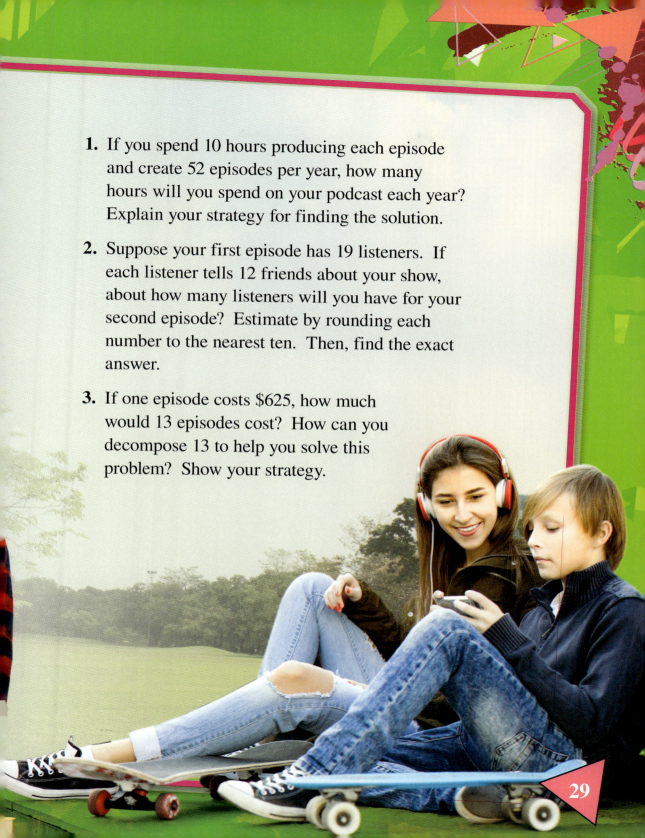

1. If you spend 10 hours producing each episode and create 52 episodes per year, how many hours will you spend on your podcast each year? Explain your strategy for finding the solution.

2. Suppose your first episode has 19 listeners. If each listener tells 12 friends about your show, about how many listeners will you have for your second episode? Estimate by rounding each number to the nearest ten. Then, find the exact answer.

3. If one episode costs $625, how much would 13 episodes cost? How can you decompose 13 to help you solve this problem? Show your strategy.

Glossary

analytics—the careful review of data or statistics

bullet journal—a customized notebook that includes a to-do list, sketchbook, list of goals, notes area, and more

consistency—the quality of staying the same at different times

entrepreneurial—the quality of being ready to start and run a business

index—the process of listing topics along with the page numbers on which they are mentioned

niche—a job or activity for a certain person or thing

profit—the gain or benefit of something

resources—supplies

sponsors—people or businesses that pay to support events, activities, or other businesses in return for the right to advertise

spreadsheet—a document with columns and rows that is used to organize information and calculate numbers

variety—a collection of different things

Virtual Assistant—someone who works online, rather than in person, to help a business owner complete a wide range of tasks

Index

analytics, 4, 24

blog, 4–5, 10, 13, 18–19, 21, 24, 27

bullet journal, 6

business lunch, 8, 21, 24

downloads, 27

microphone, 6–8, 13

Piper, 4–5, 8, 20–22, 24

Private Eye on Sci-Fi, 14, 21, 26

profit, 24

research, 6, 12, 14, 21, 24

social media, 9, 14, 21

sponsors, 12

spreadsheet, 10, 17, 21–22, 25

Virtual Assistant, 9, 21

Answer Key

Let's Explore Math

page 9:

728 megabytes per year;
14 × 52 = 500 + 200 + 20 + 8 = 728

	50	+	2
10	10 × 50 = <u>500</u>		10 × 2 = <u>20</u>
+			
4	4 × 50 = <u>200</u>		4 × 2 = <u>8</u>

page 13:

$900; 70 × 10 = 700; 70 × 2 = 140; 5 × 10 = 50; 5 × 2 = 10

page 19:

1. Total Episodes per Year: 52
2. Number of Minutes per Year: 1,560 (52 × 30 = 1,560)

page 23:

1. 180; Strategies will vary, but should include multiplying 15 × 12 = 180.
2. $375; Strategies will vary, but should include multiplying 15 × 25 = 375.

page 25:

1. 4; 250 × □ = 1,000
2. $375; 1,000 − 625 = 375

Problem Solving

1. 520 hours per year; Strategies will vary, but should include multiplying 52 × 10 = 520.
2. Estimate: 200 (20 × 10 = 200); Exact: 228 (19 × 12 = 228)
3. $8,125; Strategies will vary, but may include decomposing 13 into two addends, multiplying 625 by each addend, and then adding the products together. Possible answer: 13 = 10 + 3; 625 × 10 = 6,250; 625 × 3 = 1,875; 6,250 + 1,875 = 8,125